POEMS

IN THE

NORTH YORKSHIRE DIALECT,

BY THE LATE

JOHN CASTILLO,

JOURNEYMAN STONEMASON AND WESLEYAN REVIVALIST.

Edited, with a Memoir and Glossary, by

GEORGE MARKHAM TWEDDELL,

Fellow of the Royal Society of Northern Antiquaries, Copenhagen; Corresponding Member of the Royal Historical Society, London; Author of "Shakspere, his Times and Contemporaries," "The Bards and Authors of Cleveland and South Durham," "The People's History of Cleveland and its Vicinage," "The Visitor's Handbook to Redcar, Coatham, and Saltburn-by-the-Sea," "The History of the Stockton and Darlington Railway," &c, &c.

ROSE COTTAGE, STOKESLEY:
PUBLISHED BY THE EDITOR.
J. GOULD, PRINTER, MIDDLESBROUGH.
—
1878.

TO THE READER.

Persons having copies of Castillo's Poems in his own handwriting, will ve y much oblige the Editor by lending them to him for a time, that he may compare his own copy with them, and thus help to restore them to what Castillo intended them to be. They will be carefully returned.

Rose Cottage, Stokesley.

TO

𝕸𝖗. 𝕵𝖔𝖘𝖊𝖕𝖍 𝕯𝖆𝖑𝖊,

YEOMAN,

OF DANBY HEAD,

*One of that fast-disappearing class in our English community—
the farmers who cultivate their own land and their own brains
—I Dedicate this humble attempt to do justice to the Memory
of his departed friend, JOHN CASTILLO; hoping soon to pub-
lish a correct edition of the Local Poems of the same Author,
uniform for binding with the present pieces in the Dialect of the
District.*

GEORGE MARKHAM TWEDDELL.

Rose Cottage, Stokesley, July, 1878.

TO CASTILLO.

ALTHOUGH our creeds might vary, Castillo,
And our amusements might not be the same,
(For thou wouldst look with horror on my love
For the fine dramas with which Sophocles,
Euripides, and Terence, moved the souls
Of Greeks and Romans in the days of old ;
And those of Marlowe, Shakspere, and the rest
Of England's noblest dramatists; would scorn
To dance around the Maypole with a maid
Fair as the lily and as spotless too ;)
Yet as thou loved my Cleveland's hills and dales,
And had compassion for her people's souls,
And strove to win them from all wicked ways ;
Though thou too oft might in confusion blend
Mere innocent enjoyments with their abuse ;
I love thee, noble if mistaken soul !
And would much rather err with Puritans—
Earnest, though much too solemn—than defile
My spirit in the brutalizing pools
Of sensual debasements. And I would fain
Pay thee such honour as thou merited,
Among our Cleveland poets, though thy rank
Be not the highest : thou hast gain'd the hearts
Of numbers whom no other bard has won ;
And as the vocal songsters of the grove
Vary in compass and in melody,
Yet all are welcome to the naturalist,
So in our poesy : not Homer's strains,
Nor Dante's visits to the nether realms,
Nor Milton's soaring to eternal day,
Are for all readers. Humble lays like thine
Solace the lab'ring dalesman in his toil,
Help him to bear the numerous ills of life,
And teach his soul to look from earth to heaven.

PETER PROLETARIUS.

CONTENTS.

MEMOIR.

John Castillo was born at Rathfarnum, three miles from Dublin, in the year 1792; his parents, like the great majority of the people of Ireland, being Roman Catholics; an obnoxious state — church doing more than anything else to retard the enlightenment of the people. Ireland at that time nominally possessed two houses of parliament of its own; but as the so-called representatives of the Irish people were exclusively elected by a handful of Protestants, and many of these members were in the pay of the British government, which for centuries ruled the Emerald Isle with a rod of iron, the entire extinction of that parliament eight years later was no great loss to the country. Sir Hercules Langrishe had, indeed, in the year of Castillo's birth, succeeded in carrying a bill to allow Roman Catholics to practice the law, and removing certain restrictions on education, trade, and inter-marriages; but when the Dublin merchants petitioned for the restoration of the elective franchise, and other civil rights, to Roman Catholics, a Mr. Latouche moved that their request be rejected, and his motion was carried by a large majority.

The mischievous interference of governments in theology has in all ages caused immense crime and misery; and until mankind come to regard religion as a thing entirely between themselves and their Heavenly Father, with which no human authority has the least right to interfere, and mere speculative opinions as matters for which no man is to be called to account by his fellow-man, much less to be made to suffer pains and penalties, there can be no real civil and religious liberty; and without civil and religious liberty no people can be truly happy. Under the cloak of religion, spoliation and persecution, generation after generation, were perpetrated on the poor population of that noble island, whose savage kerns, under proper government, might have been developed into one of the finest peoples on this planet.

> "'Tis well to cultivate each yard of soil
> For corn, and fruits, and flowers; it is well
> To probe the earth for minerals that may
> Be fused to human use; but it is vain
> To prate of 'wealth of nations' in our pride—
> Yea, bloated ignorance—if we despise,

MEMOIR.

"Neglect, or scorn, the meanest child that's born
Of meanest parents; for there is a wealth
To b¹ developed by all nations yet,
In whose bright rays all other wealth will pale."

                                    PETER PROLETARIUS.

Under such misgovernment, Irishmen could not entertain feel-
ings of friendship for England, and many of them had enlisted
into the armies of France, fighting against her for despotic kings,
whilst others were amongst the best soldiers in the army of
American Independence. And when Castillo was born there was
a ferment throughout Europe. France, just risen, like a mighty
giant, from eight centuries of cruel oppression, was bravely defy-
ing the world for that liberty which, when gotten, she knew not
how best to use: so that in Ireland, as elsewhere, the oppressed
looked to her for succour; whilst timid reformers in England
were scared by some French excesses into bolstering up all the
rottenness and wrong-doing of their own government, some of
them, like Burke, becoming more rabid than those who had
always been opposed to all reform. The history of Ireland at
the time of Castillo's birth is a subject I would strongly recom-
mend my readers to study, as we even yet know far too little of
the sister kingdom. No wonder that Castillo's parents should
leave their oppressed country, where tortures on the one hand,
and secret conspiracies on the other, were the order of the day;
a country of which an able Irishman, GEORGE HOLMES,* a few

* SKETCHES IN SOME OF THE SOUTHERN COUNTIES ON IRELAND, COL-
LECTED DURING A TOUR IN THE AUTUMN, 1797, IN A SERIES OF LET-
TERS, is a delightful octavo volume, published in London in 1801. The
work is illustrated with beautiful views of the interior of the Abbey of
Holy Cross, the cathedral-crowned Rock of Cashel, Cormac's Chapel on
the south side of the said cathedral, Ross Castle, Mucruss Lake, and Lis-
more Castle, etc., from his own pencil; and the sixteen Letters of which
the volume is composed are not only most pleasant reading, but are full of
historical and archæological information, both his father and himself being
well versed in antiquities. The book was dedicated to the Duchess of
Devonshire, and was the means of procuring for him the patronage of the
Dukes of Leinster and of Devonshire, Viscount de Vesci, and others of the
nobility, in his profession as an artist, which he came to England to prac-
tice in 1802, though, I believe, the rightful heir to an Irish peerage and to
immense lauded possessions As a proof of George Holme's assertion,
quoted above, of the general ignorance of readers regarding Ireland, I may
mention that Sterne, who was born at Clonmel, November 24, 1713, but
left the country in his boyhood, takes a SENTIMENTAL JOURNEY to the foot
of Mount Taurira, in France, for a pleasing picture of a peasant's dance
after supper, which then, as I learn from good George Holmes's valuable
volume, he might have found in his native country, and which the artist-
author saw and described some thirty years after the body of Sterne had
been stolen from its grave in "the new burying-ground near Tyburn," and
dissected by Professor Collignon at the university of Cambridge, and his
skeleton strung together with wires for the instruction of students in
anatomy.

years later remarked :—" Strange to say, Ireland, which, for a
space of six hundred years and more, has been politically con-
nected with, and continues to be a powerful and valuable gem in,
the crown of Great Britain, is less known to the people of Eng-
land, in general, than the most remote regions."

On their voyage from Ireland to England, the Castillo family
were shipwrecked at the Isle-of-Man ; and, when the subject of
this memoir was in his second or third year, settled at the quiet
hamlet of Lealholm Bridge—nine miles from Whitby, thirteen
from Gisbro', and eighteen from Stokesley. If, like Napper
Tandy, and others, he found it necessary to leave his country to
escape political prosecution, which is by no means unlikely, I do
not know how he could have chosen a safer or more sequestered
spot than the Lealholm of that day. Thus from his earliest re-
collections, though by birth and parentage Irish, John Castillo
was a resident of Lealholm Bridge ; and, though often obliged to
leave his foster-valley, "to beg a brother of the earth to give
him leave to toil," as BURNS very pithily puts it, the principal
part of his life was spent in that rural hamlet, his residence being
the humble stone cottage adjoining the old papermill. Thus in
his "Lealholm Bridge—a Soliloquy during a Visit, after some
years' absence," we have :—

> " In distant lands my father's lot was cast,
> And we were left to feel the bitter blast.
> Death's fatal hand its victim did arrest,
> And tore him from the darlings of his breast.
> I, by a mother's care, when young, was led
> Down by the river to yon primrose bed,
> Where birds so sweetly sung the trees among,
> I thought those days were happy, bright, and long.
> Oft I, a boy, with others of my age,
> Did eager here in youthful sports engage :
> Oft in yon wood we roved when life was new,
> The rocks, and trees, and rugged caves to view,
> Where woodbines wild with sweets perfumed the air,
> And all seem'd joyous, beautiful, and fair."

Glaisdale, in which Lealholm Bridge is situated, was until re-
cently a chapelry to Danby, but is now, by an order in council,
erected into a separate vicarage. Between there and Whitby is a
population amongst which Protestants say the light of the Re-
formation has never fairly penetrated, but which the Castillos
would regard as remaining loyal to the only true church. It was
wise of his mother to lead him forth in childhood to see the
beauty of the green fields, and golden whins, and purple ling, in
their seasons ; to listen to the song of birds, to gather wild
flowers on the banks of the Esk—a river whose Celtic name
carries one back to the times of the ancient Britons ; and well

would it have been for poor Castillo if he had but possessed some
kind and intelligent friend capable of leading him to commune
with Nature, and of teaching him to despise that soul-blighting
Superstition which is sacrificed to in all quarters, but has its most
devoted worshippers in sequestered dales like the Danby* of Cas-
tillo's time. As it was, he had fearful dreams of "an ocean of
troubled liquid fire," at a time when such deleterious teaching
ought never to have reached his childish ears ; and he "saw a
number of tormented and tormenting beings, most of which were
in human shape, rolling about, tossed by those dismal and furious
waves, and as soon as some sunk, others arose, full of horror and
dismal wailings," in visions which ought to have been redolent
of the beauty and perfume of flowers, and the music of birds and
brooks. The humblest psychologist who glances through the
writings of poor Castillo will at once perceive the baleful effects
which the popular superstitions have had on what, under proper
culture, would have been a great intellect. Some day we may
discover, that the true development of our future men and women,
mentally, morally, and physically, is the only sound political
economy, and the surest way to augment "the wealth of nations."
For, as Sir WILLIAM JONES has well sung, in his famous Ode in
imitation of Alcæus :—

"What constitutes a state ?
Not high-rais'd battlement or labour'd mound,
      Thick wall or moated gate ;
Not cities proud with spires and turrets crown'd ;
      Not bays and broad-arm'd ports,
Where, laughing at the storm, rich navies ride ;
      Not starr'd and spangled courts,
Where low-brow'd baseness wafts perfume to pride.
      No : men, high-minded men,
With powers as far above dull brutes endued
      In forest, brake, or den,
As beasts excel cold rocks and brambles rude ;
      Men who their duties know,
But know their rights, and, knowing, dare maintain,

* Thank God, we have at last got a railroad through the dale; and I
know of no pleasanter railway ride than on the line foolishly called North
Yorkshire and Cleveland,—just as though Cleveland was not a portion of
the North Riding. Danby and its neighbouring dales is a district rich in
the remains of Scandinavian folk-lore. The following communication,
from a late respected member for the North Riding, speaks for itself.—

"11, Dean's Yard, Westminster, May 7, 1861.

"Sir,—I shall be happy to be a subscriber to your work on Cleveland as
described in your prospectus. I hope it may include the district of Danby-
dale, where I suspect the traditions must be curious, both in the way of
language, customs, and sports.—Your faithful servant,

"G M. Tweddell, Esq."   "E. S CAYLEY."

> Prevent the long-aim'd blow,
> And crush the tyrant while they rend the chain:
> These constitute a state,
> And sov'reign Law that state's collected will,
> O er thrones and globes elate
> Sits empress, crowning good, repressing ill."

When about eleven or twelve years of age, he lost his father, who had sent him to school, and taken him to hear mass (like a good Catholic), and given him such training as he was capable of giving. But the now fatherless lad must leave school, like tens of thousands of lads in the present day, just when he is beginning to imbibe a little book-learning, and (as the Cleveland folks say) "he mun try te mak a bit scrat for hiz awn living!" Castillo was what my Lancashire friends call "punced up:" we must not wonder, then, if he is slightly intolerant to all who do not see with his eyes. Leaving Lealholm Bridge on the death of his father, he went, as servant boy, with a gentleman into Lincolnshire, where he spent two years, and then returned to his adopted valley, where he learnt the art and mystery of a stone mason, and became converted amongst the Wesleyan Methodists;—being admitted into class, April 5, 1818, at the chapel at Danby End, when he was some twenty-six years old: and to the end of his life he was an energetic revivalist amongst that body, through all his poverty and privations. Thus, in "A Farewell," he sings:—

> "From a land full of friends where he covets to stay,
> Poor tost-about Castillo 's forced far away,
> Into regions beyond, where his lot may be cast,
> So he leaves this small tribute, which may be his last.
>
> How happy is he who has work to abide,
> With his child on his knee, by his own fireside!
> Where he 's cheer'd with the counsel and charms of a wife,
> To lessen or share in the troubles of life.
>
> 'T is but few who the ills of the traveller know
> While to rivers and hills relating his woe,
> Far away from his friends, and out of employ,
> With no one to share in his trouble or joy.
>
> While he sees some for wickedness highly extoll'd,
> He is sharing the frowns of a hard-hearted world;
> Receives for his good deeds a sad recompence,
> A stranger, a lodger, and all on expense!
>
> Yet there 's One who, if he will his follies control,
> Will preserve both the health of his body and soul:
> To the married or single, the husband or wife,
> RELIGION can sweeten the bitters of life!"

And in " The Lodger in Liverpool, or the Mason in Winter nipt by the Frost, while a Card-party were enjoying themselves in an adjoining Room," he looks back with longing love to dear old Cleveland, which he had been forced to leave in the battle for bread :—

> " While sad I sit, oft musing over
> Happy days for ever fled ;
> A lonely lodger in a corner,
> Like some hermit in his shed.
>
> All around seems blithe and merry ;
> My light 's dim and heart 's unstrung,
> While memory turns to yonder valley,
> On whose flowery banks I 've sung.
>
> Dirty, ragged, and down-hearted,
> Far from country, friends, and home ;
> And as far from kindness parted,
> Doom'd for work the world to roam.
>
>   *   *   *
>
> But when time makes all surrender,
> Nor permits the least excuse,
> Happy they whom time's avenger
> Charges not with its abuse."

Strange that nations professing the sublimest of all religions, Christianity, and boasting of their superior civilization, cannot see that there must be something radically wrong in the very constitution of society where men, able and willing to work at the most useful employments, are doomed to starve, for no fault of their own ; unable to make an honest livelihood with comfort, even when, like poor Castillo, they have neither wife nor child to maintain ; and, unless wanted for, and willing to do, the devil's work of war, are blasphemously designated a "surplus population." As the gifted ETA MAWR sang, half a century ago, in her excellent "Ode to Wealth " :—

> " Oh, Poverty ! be thou my fate,
> And the worst ills that on thee wait,
> If e'er I raise my truant voice,
> To call thee, though in jest, my choice !
> Does Virtue shoot her trembling rays ?
> Thy hand extinguishes the blaze.
> Does Genius fire the peasant's soul ?
> It withers at thy stern control ;
> Or if it burst its kindling way,
> As rends the cloud the light'ning's ray,
> Ah ! how shall he, whose soul refined
> Has roam'd the raptured heights of mind,
> Descend from genius' lofty ken,
> To herd him with his fellow-men ?
> If courted in his humble sphere,
> By those to fame and fortune dear,
> What double wretchedness shall wait
> The contrast of his adverse fate !
> To see delights he must not share—
> His evil with their good compare—

And from the castle's splendid walls,
And its gay mirth-resounding halls,
Back to his straw-built shed to steal,
And feel—as only bards can feel!"

In the months of January and February, 1837, Castillo caught
a succession of colds, which, added to previous hardships, brought
on influenza; and he never afterwards was the strong man whose
brawny arm had hewn out and dressed the freestone of the Cleve-
land hills, happy if he could but earn daily bread by his hard
toil, and assist in the labours of the sect with which he had allied
himself. That year, on his partial recovery, he was invited during
the summer to Stockton-on-Tees, with a brother revivalist, "but,"
says he, "we carried rather too coarse metal for that refined
place,"—methodism always changing its character when wealthy
folks join the society. In the dales, however, Castillo was a suc-
cessful revivalist. In February, 1838, he set out for the Pickering
circuit. "Finding," says he, "the channels at home (if I have
a home) in some measure blocked up, I went away, in the storm
of 1838, but not having my name on any plan as a preacher, I
occasionally got severe lashes on that account; but endeavoured,
as much as possible, to keep out of the pulpits, by holding prayer
meetings, and giving exhortations out of the singing-pews, or
from the forms:" and, I presume, it is in allusion to some of
those revivalist doings that he remarks, in his "Village
Preaching":—

"Far over Cleveland's lofty hills,
Water'd by rivulets and rills,
A lovely village doth appear,
And o'er the trees its chimneys rear.
A church there is without a steeple,
And several unconverted people;
Though not much pious fruit appear,
The people still desire to hear:
To chapel oft they go and back,
In their old summer-beaten track.

*   *   *

The forms were set, and rostrum fixt,
The preacher went, and took his text.

*   *   *

Having, as he thought, clear'd his way,
They sang, and then began to pray.
He left his elevated station,
And went among his congregation.

*   *   *

But such unusual proceeding
They say completely spoil'd the meeting:
That preacher's conduct is unstable,
Who cannot keep behind the table!

*   *   *

> If I should go that way once more,
> And find the people as before,
> They must have either chain or cable,
> If they keep me behind the table."

Castillo died at Pickering, April 16, 1845, at the age of fifty-three. With all the vigour of an ancient Puritan, he was cramped in mind by most of the narrowness that rendered Puritanism intolerable to the people of England in the days of my illustrious ancestor, the Lord Protector. Thus we have, as the title of one of his rhyming dialogues, " The Music Band is all the go, but it is a plausible and successful snare of the devil." In his verses on " The Wedding," the " bands of music, singing, dancing, and drinking," are condemned as though bad in themselves ; jollity being a crime in his eyes, even though it was unaccompanied by excess ; and in his " Broad and Narrow Way," he says :—

> " With pleasant walks and cheerful company,
> And harmless games—if harmless games there be."

" Merry Christmas, as kept in England," in the nineteenth century, was as great an abomination to poor Castillo as the old English May-games were to Philip Stubs in 1595, or to the Rev. Thomas Hall, B.D., of King's Norton, in 1660 ; neither of whom could have read Herrick's beautiful verses, " Corinna's going a-Maying," without almost going into fits. And as for the theatre, why all who frequented such places, though it might be to listen to the unequalled plays of Shakspere from the lips of the greatest actors of the day, were vile and accurst. Unlike the generality of dissenters, who generally make Good Friday a day for tea-meetings and rejoicings, Castillo had a peculiar veneration for the day set apart to commemorate the death of the Holy Jesus ; and he even believed that the two *sinkers* who were dragged out of a coal pit, one of them killed, and the other dreadfully wounded, when

> " The kibble kick'd, brim-full of splinter'd rock,"

were punished by " the just judgment of an angry God " for going down to work on that holy day.

Castillo's most popular poem is " Awd Abzaak," which gives us a graphic picture of a Sunday in the Dales at the commencement of the present century. His style is evidently patterned after that adopted by Burns, from Fergusson and the older Scottish poets, and made familiar to Cleveland readers by the inspired ploughboy. It originally consisted of the first part only, which is superior in literary execution to the portion afterwards added.

Old Isaac Hobb, who used to live near Glaisdale Chapel (now church), is supposed to have been the lay figure, so to speak, from which Castillo first delineated the picture he has painted for us, but the sentiment of the piece is principally drawn from his own experience. Some will regard him as the true exponent of saving grace; and others, like a literary correspondent of mine in Switzerland (the late James Dixon, LL.D.), as "a religious bigot"; but all must admire his fearlessly honest expression of opinion, and the ability he has displayed in depicting his rustic compeers.

The greatest merit of Castillo as a writer is his quiet humour: with his theology I have nothing to do. Claiming the right to think and speak freely for myself, I must allow the same privilege to others. To talk of "tolerating" one from whom our opinions may differ in speculative matters, is simply impertinent. I *have* to do with my fellow man's morality, because it bears on my happiness and that of my neighbours and friends : what his religious opinions are is no more my business, or that of others, than his estimate of Wordsworth as a poet, or any other subject on which we have a right to converse as friends, if we feel so inclined, but certainly not to seize each other as it were by the throat, and demand of each other, as though we must be enemies if we cannot both see with the same eyes.

I only met poor Castillo once, and that was during my apprenticeship. He had his poem of the "Pickerin' Steeple Chass" in manuscript, which he read to me, with some other unpublished pieces. I at once singled out the lines commencing

"To see 'em all seea blahth an' merry,"

as the best of all that he had read to me ; and, on going through the printed poem, I still regard them as the most original and vigorous in the piece; and it was through my recommendation that he retained them in the printed copies, when some Wesleyan preacher whom he had consulted had got him persuaded to expunge them. He was very much pleased with my criticism, but the minister's opinion seemed to weigh with him. But when I told him that probably his reverend friend knew more about theology than poetry, and evidently, as a believer in a personal devil, was taking literally what was merely figurative, he at once agreed with me, and before parting promised that the lines should stand. Castillo's great want through life was a friend who was alike well versed in the art of poetry and master of the North York Dialect. Those who "improved" his pieces, as they thought, by refining them, only made matters worse. It reminds me of the editor of a newspaper to whom I once gave a Dialect poem of Florence Cleveland's for insertion. " It is a good piece," said he, " but we must *correct* this "—pointing to one of the truest touches in it—" for it is *bad* grammar ! "   " If you make it grammatical," was my reply, " it will cease to be a true specimen of the Dialect."   Many seem to think that they illustrate a Dialect by writing good English, and knocking out a few general words here and there, and inserting local words instead.   They might as well think to build a Grecian temple by removing the freestone and inserting a few blocks of marble in the outside walls of a Gothic abbey.   I have earnestly endeavoured to restore the text of Castillo to its primitive purity—for every previous editor has made it worse than before—and I have only made such alterations as he would himself have approved of,—such, in fact, as I thought absolutely necessary to give him a permanent niche in that small temple which is quite large enough to contain the few true delineators of our North York Dialect, now fast going, as all Dialects must go, but the memory of which ought not to be buried with them.

Rose Cottage, Stokesley.

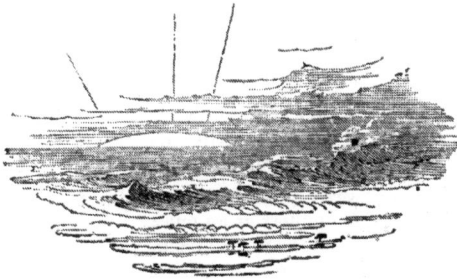

Tailpiece by Linton.

AWD AHZAAK.

PAIT FOST.

YAH neet az Ah went heeam fra' wark,
A lahtle bit afooar 't waz dark,
Quite blahth an' cheerful az a lark
    Ah thowt me-sel';
An' sat mah down, te rist a bit,
    At top o' t' hill.

Fooaks just wer tonnin' oot ther ky
A lahtle plain awd man com by :—
"Cum sit ye doon, gud frinnd," sez I,
    " An' rist yer legs " :
He 'd been a bit o' floor te buy,
    An' tweea 'r three eggs.

Ah fand him varra gud te stop ;—
Hiz staff he set up as a prop ;—
Hiz hooary heead he lifted up,
    An' thus cumpleean'd :—
(Sum fragments ov a gud-like feeace,
    Ther yıt remeean'd.)

"Yoo see," sez he, "mah deer yung frinnd,
Mah travel 's ommost at an end ;
Wi' age me back begins te bend,
    An' white 's me hair ;
Ov this warld's griefs, yoo may depend,
    Ah 've had me share."

Hiz teeal, thoff simple, it wer grand,
An' varra gud te understand,—
Hiz stick steead up aboon hiz hand
    T' awd fashin'd way ;
Hiz cooat an' hat wer weather-tann'd,
    A duffil grey.

B

"Ah think," sez Ah, " 'at 't Scripter sez,
Grey hairs is honourable driss,
If tha be fund i' reeteousniss,
    Be faith obtain'd ;
An' Ah think, be what yer leeaks express,
    That prahz yoo 've gain'd.

Wi' age it izzent gud te joke,
An' 't 'z ommost owwer warm te woke ;
Sit doon, an' hev a bit o' toke,
    O' things at 'z past :
Awd men, like yoo, hev seeaf beeath heeard
    An' seen a vast."

" A vast Ah hev beeath heeard an' seen,
An' felt m'sfotten's arrows keen,
Az yoo remark, whahl Ah hev been
    On this life's stage ;
It 's sike a varra changin' scene,
    Fra youth te age.

Hoo greeat, an' yet hoo feeble's man !
Hiz life at langest 's bud a span ; "
Hiz history he thus began,
    Wi' tears te tell ;
An' if yer ears be owt like mahn,
    'T will pleease ye weel.

" Lang sahn Ah lost me wife," sez he,
" Which was a heavy cross te me ;
An' then me sun teeak off tit sea,
    A fahn young man,—
An' Ah neea mair hiz feeace mun see,
    It 's ten te yan.

Ah happen'd te be off yah day,
A kahnd ov sweethart, az tha say,
Com in an' teeak me lass away,
    Wiv howsin stuff ;
An' noo, poor thing, she 's deead, tha say,
    A lang way off !

It 's noo neen year, an' gannin' i' ten,
Sen Ah at t' barkwood join'd sum men,
'T waz there Ah fell an leeam'd me-sen,
    I' spite o' care :
An' fooast te give up ther an' then,
    An' work neea mair.

Bud t' nighbers hez been varra gud,
Or else lang sahn Ah 'd stuck i' t' mud,
An' seea throo them, an' t' help o' God,
  Ah gits me breead ;
Ah howp they 'll be rewarded for 't
  When Ah 'z loa laid :

Bud, seeing all me cumfots gone,
Ah diddent knaw what way te ton ;
Then Ah began te sigh an' mon
  Beeath neet an'.day :
Ah bowt a Bahble, an' began —
  Te read an' pray.

An' az Ah read, an' az Ah pray'd,
Ah thowt it thunner'd owwer me heead,
An' offens Ah wer sadly flay'd
  Wi' dismal noises :
Sumtahms i' bed Ah thowt Ah heeard
  Mysterious voices.

A preeacher chanced te cum this way,—
Ah 've koase te ivver bliss that day
Kahnd Providence led me that way
  This man te hear :
Ah, like a sheep, had geean astray
  Fer monny a year.

He sed 't waz luv o' Christ cumpell'd him,—
Bud seean az ivver Ah beheld him,
Ah thowt 'at sum kahnd frinnd had teld him
  All me hart ;
Fer ivvery wod, like arrows pointed,
  Meead it smart.

Ah thowt, tell then, 'at Ah waz reet,
Bud he set me sins all i' me seet ;
At last Ah fell doon at his feet,
  Wi' solid grief ;
Ah thowt Ah sud hev deed afoor
  Ah fund relief.

Ah really thowt, if you'll believe ma,
'At hell waz oppen te receeave ma ;
Sum sed the Lord wad seean relieve ma,
  He waz me keeper ;
Bud all they sed did nowt but greeve ma,—
  It cut ma deeper.

Ah dreeaded the Almighty's froon,
Ah wander'd greetin' up an' doon,
Nowther i' cuntry nor i' toon
    Neea rist Ah fand;
Me sins, like stars, did´me surroond,
    Or heeaps o' sand.

At t' thowts o' ivverlasting pains,
An' being bun' iv endless cheeans,
Me bleead, like ice, ran thruff me veins,
    Wi' shivverin' dreead;
Ah cuddent sleep, an' Ah fergat
    Te eeat me breead.

Then varra seean t' repooat waz raized,
An' all round t' village it wer bleeazed,
Awd Ahzaak, he waz gannin' craized,
    An' nowt seea seer;
Mah cottage then, fer days an' days,
    Neea sowl com near.

At last this gud man com ageean,
Fer which me hart waz glad an' fain,
Just like a thosty land fer rain,
    Ah sat quite near him,
Whahl ivv'ry organ ov me soul,
    Waz bent te hear him.

But seean az Ah that sarmon heer'd,
A still small voice me sperits cheer'd,
An' Ah, that varra neet, waz meead,
    A happy man;
Te praise the Lord, wi' all me hart,
    Ah then began.

Ah knew He had me sins forgeen,
Whahl Ah had in His prizence been,
An' that Hiz bleead cud wesh ma clean,
    An' white az snaw,
An' mak ma fit wi' Him te raign,
    Whahl here belaw.

Sen that, i' all me conflicts here,
Ah flees te Him wi' faith an' prayer,
An' He, i' marsy, lens an ear,
    Thruff Hiz dear Son;
An' this iz t' way, wi' howp an' fear,
    Ah travils on.

Oft, when Ah thus draws near te Him,
He maks me e'es wi' tears te swim,
Then fills me hart quite up tit brim,
    Wi' t' luv o' God ;
An' when Ah gits mair faith i' Him,
    Ah hods me hod !

Sumtahms ah 've had yon beck te swim,
An' monny a tahm this hill te clim',
Wi' heavy hart an' weary lim',
    An' sweeaty broo ;
Bud all 'at Ah can trust Him in,
    He helps ma throo.

Iv all the straits o' life," sez he,
" Howivver bare me cubbert be,
Wi' brown breead crusts, an' wormwood tea,
    Or even gall ;
Wherivver Ah finnds Christ te be,
    He sweetens all.

Me nighbers all, Ah dearly luv 'em,
An' oft Ah 'z fooast fer te repruv 'em,
To seeak the Lord Ah tries te muv 'em,
    Wi' hart sincere ;
Bud t' ansers oft 'at Ah gets frev 'em,
    Iz quite severe.

Ah 've oft felt sorry te me-sel',
Beeath grieved an' shamm'd t' trewth te tell,
When Ah hev heeard our awd kirk bell
    Ring in te prayer ;
Ah 's flay'd 'at sum el hear 't i' hell
    Upbreead 'em there.

They'll sit or lig upon ther deead,
An' toke aboot all kahnds o' trade,
An' laff, an lee, quite undismay'd,
    Tell tha 've rung in ;
Sike fooaks, tit warld tha 're owther wed
    Or near akin.

Sum sez ther priest 'z a stumlin'-block,
He nivver leads 'em on tit rock,
Like thooase 'at mends a threead-bare frock
    Wi' a new piece ;
He cares bud lahtle fer hiz flock,
    If he gits t' fleece.

Bud oors, he iz a Christian breet,
He preeaches Christ wi' all his meet,
Fills eeach believer wiv deleet
     'At gans te hear him;
An' therefooar ov hiz people's bleead
     The truth el clear him.

Ah 've heerd him tell 'em, pat an' plain,
'At they mun all be *booarn ageean,*
Or suffer ivverlastın' pain,
     I' t' warld te cum;
Bud if they 'll flee te Christ i' tahm,
     Fer all ther 's rooam.

I' t' pulpit, or i' conversashin,
Hez awlus on for t' soul's salvashin,
Wi' kahnd repreeaf or exhooatashin,
     Or coonsil sweet;
An' thooase 'at follow hiz perswashin,
     They 'll be reet.

An' yıt Ah 'z flay'd, if t' trewth waz knooan,
There 's monny a precious soul i' pawn,
Fer that gud seed 'at he hez sawn ,
     Without effect;
An' t' bleeam fer ivver iz ther awn,
     Thruff sad neglect.

Thare 's sum 'at sez—(bud they 're misteean)
When tha 're baptahz'd tha 're booan ageean;
Just here tha miss t' foundashin steean,
     An' builds i' t' sand;
An' tha 've neea dreead, till t' house iz doon,
     Bud it will stand.

Ah 've knawn yung men, an' wimmin too,
An' men wi' t' hair all off ther broo,
Afooar he 'z read hiz lessons throo
     'Z been fast asleep;
Whahl udders that far better knew,
     'Z been seen te weep.

They 'll rock an' riggle like a ship,
Till sum kahnd frinnd giz them a nip,
Or wacken'd up wi' t' saxon's whip,
     Or others koffin :
Then, mebby when tha 've rubb'd ther e'en,
     Tha 'll start a laffin.

Sum 'z lived te three or fowwer skooar,
An' 'z lang tahm here had rulin' poor ;
Tha 've wooan deep tracks across yon moor
    Wi' constant gannin';
Bud still, all t' whahl, for this warld's geer
    Ther harts wer langin'.

Thersels tha 've nivver fairly seen,
Tha 've nivver knooan ther sins fergeen,
Tho' monny a tahm ther pray'rs hev been
    Az loud az t' clark ;
Fer all tha 've had tweea pair ov een,
    Tha 've deed i' t' dark.

Ther's sum 'at t' neeam o' Christian beers,
'An 'z had that neeam fer monny years,
'At 'z berried owwer heead an' ears
    I' wardly care ;
An' oft at kirk, we 've cause te fear
    Tha markit there.

Ah wer at a sarten hoose yah day,
An' t' awd man tiv hiz sun did say,
'If all be weel, thou mun away
    Temooan tit kirk ;
An' try te git our reet next week,
    Te cum te wark.

An' Tommy, he 'z i' sike a tackin',
That cooat al spoil for want o' mackin',
If t' taylear 'z theer, thou mun be at him
    Te cum an' all ;
That 'z weel contrahved, an' then yah thrang
    Al deea fer all.

Thou need n't stop te gan' round t' fahm,
Thou 'll hea te be there i' reet gud tahm,
Or mebby, if tha dizzent mahnd,
    Thou 'll loss the chance ;
There 'z sumtahms three or fowwer at him
    All at yance.

It 'z owwer far te gan afeeat,
An' if 't be warm thou 's seer te sweeat,
The mudder, she 'll deea nowt bud freeat,
    Seea tak awd Dragon ;
An' tell t' reet he mun cum next week,
    Te mend our waggon.'

Then if ye chance, i' t' cooase o' t' weeak,
O' t' Sunday's subject fer te speeak,
You'll finnd awd memory seea weeak,
  It 'z all fergitten;
Thus wounded souls 'at 'z been hawf heeal'd
  T' awd sarpent 'z bitten.

That skull 'at 'z mowlded green an' gray,
T' awd saxon dag up t' udder day,
Knaws varra neer az mitch az they,
  O' t' Sunday's sarmon;
You may az weel o' t' subject toke
  Te sum awd Garman.

That poor awd man 'z noo deead an' geean,.
It 'z hard te say what way he 'z teean,
'At use te stand ageean t' funt steean,
  Te tak fooaks' watches;
Whahl careless lads i' t' singing pew,
  Wer cuttin natches.

Fer want o' proper cultivashin,
They shuffle on without salvashin,
A vast, Ah 'z flay'd, hez this perswashin,
  Beeath yung an' awd,—
Te be fergeen they hev neea cashin
  Tell deead and kawd!

Tha 'll finn'd it oot afoor 't be lang,
'At tha 've all t' tahm been sadly wrang,
Ther will's may then be owwer strang
  Te breeak or bend;
An' noo tha say tha 're owwer thrang,
  Tha can't attend.

I' Summer tahm tha 'll leeave t 'awd nest,
An' driss up i' ther varra best,
An' gallop off alang wi' t' rist,
  Te t' fair or reeaces;
A vast gits what tha nivver kest,
  At sike like pleeaces.

Ther 's sum gits theer wi' wooden legs on,
Monny poor awd men wi' wigs on,
Sarves t' yung fooaks te run ther rigs on,
  A fahn example;
Whahl doon i' t' dust ther poor awd lims,
  Sumtahmes tha trample!

Ther 's sum can nowther sit nor lig,
Aboot t' elecshins, they 're seea big ;
Tha say they 're Britons rump an' rig,
　　　But wheea can trist 'em,
When frev a Tory tiv a Whig
　　　A glass al twist 'em.

Ther 's sum 'at 's rayder shooat o' seet,
Fer t' seeak o' tweea 'r three sov'rans breet,
Giz in ther vooat, an' thinks it reet,
　　　Fer t' Roman stranger ;
Udders plaisters up i' t' street,—
　　　T' Chetch is i' Danger !

An' seea tha yan prevent annudder,
Wi' sike like polytical bother,
Tho' t' best ov all can't seeave his brudder,
　　　Nor ransom him ;
That spark 'at 's left they try te smudder
　　　Wi' stratagem

Az for thooase Metbodys, tha say,
Tha mak seea varra mitch te deea,
Ther's sum wad deea nowt else bud pray,
　　　An' read, an' preeach,
Till tha git all meead Methodys
　　　Within ther reeach !

Bud thare waz neean ov this amaze,
I' neean ov oor fooarfayther's days,
Thoff ther gud deeds an' honest prayers,
　　　An' pious readins,
Hez been, neea doot, az good az thayers,
　　　Wi' all ther meetins.

Te see 'em doon o' beeath ther knees,
I' t' kirk, or t' field, or onder trees,
Wi' brokken harts an' teerful e'es,
　　　Wer quite uncommon ;
An' if tha hevvent deed i' t' faith,
　　　Then what's cumm'd on em ?

Te preeach 'em all geean doon te hell,
It is a dreeadful teeal te tell,
An' we mun wi' oor kindred dwell,
　　　Seea we, like them,
Will on life's ooashin tak wer chance,
　　　An' sink or swim.

Tha mak sike wark amang t' yung fooaks,
Tha breeak up all wer jooavil spooats,
Tha thin wer ranks, an' storm wer pooats,
      Wi' strange confushin;
Ther 'z nowt bud we mun cry't all doon,
      A mere delushin.

Bud uz 'at seldom hev attendid,
Tha deea n't git uz seea eeasy mendid,
An awd stiff yack 's nut eeasy bendid,
      That's varra trew ;
Bud thooase 'at weean't bend, yoo see,
      Mun breeak enoo.

Sumtahmes, when pashin' let 'em in,
Wi' wods te sweerin' near akin,
Fer fear that t' sad effecks o' sin,
      Ther harts sud hardin,
Tha try te rub off ther an' then,
      Wi' axin' pardin.

Tha trifle on fra' year te year,
Like watches wooan oot o' repair,
Thoff if tha wad, it 's varra clear,
      Tha mud be mendid :
Bud they perceeav neea danger near,
      Tell life is ended.

Awd Sattan seea pollutes ther mahnd,
They weea n't stoop tit means disahnd,
Till t' hairspring gits wi't'mainspring twahnd,
      An' seea hard coll'd,
Tha 're fooast away te git refahnd,
      I' t' udder wolld.

He leeads sum on like mountebanks,
Az stright az thoff tha ran o' planks,
An' tells 'em, i' ther jooavil pranks,
      He'll nut deceeave 'em ;—
Tell on awd Jordan's stormy banks,
      Ther cumfots leeave 'em.

He leeads sum on annudder way,
An' whispers te them neet an' day,
'At they need nowder read nor pray,
      They 've deean nowt wrang ;
Or if they hev, he'll set it reet,
      Afooar 't be lang !

Ther 's udders oft been iv alarm,
Bud, Felix like, when t' hart wer warm,
He's sed, Gan,' an' sum udder tahm
  Ah 'll send fer thee ;
When tha that tahm, tha diddent knaw
  Mud ivver see.

Tha rob ther sowls ov ther awn reet,
Tha really winnot cum te t' leet,
Lest o' ther sins tha git a seet,
  An' sud be seeaved,
An' be ov all ther plishers sweet
  At yance bereeaved.

Tell deep sunk down i' t' bonning lake,
Tha then begin te fear an' quake,
Where vengeance can neea pitty tak,
  Which there hez sent 'em ;
Bud furious feeands i' horrid shap,
  Mun there torment 'em !

Tha leeak fer sum yan te delivver,
Bud there they 'll finnd neea comfot nivver,
There tha mun weep an' wail fer ivver,
  Ther harvist's past ;
Ther summer 's ended. refuge fails 'em,
  An' tha 're lost.

Whahl life danced on her silver springs,
Tha lafft at Deeath an' seerous things,—
Scooan'd Heaven, its proffits, priests an' kings,
  An' felt neea sham :
That tha deean't noo wi' angils sing,
  Thersels tha bleeam !

Ther dreeadful doom an' destiny
Let us git all we can te flee,
Be preeachin' Christ where'er we be,
  I' deed an' wod ;
Tell all wer frinnds ther folly see,
  An' ton te God.

Ah 've been i' t' way noo seeaven year,"
An' as he spak a brahny tear
Ran doon eeach cheeak, az crystal clear,
  Fra owder e'e ;
" Thenk God ! Ah feel, whahl Ah sit here,
  It's weel wi' me.

Bud t' neet is cummin' on amain,
An' 't leeaks az if 't was boon te rain,
Or else mah stooary's nut hawf deean,
    'At Ah 've te tell ;
Bud mebby we may meet ageean,—
    Till then, Fareweel ! "

Thoff he had all thooase sorrows booan,
Composer in eeach feeater shooan.
Thoff he 'd te walk an' live alooan,
    Fra day te day ;
Ah wish'd hiz keeas had been me awn,
    An' kom away.

T' END O' T' FOST PAIT.

Tailpiece by Bewick.

PAIT SECOND.

WIV HIS DEEIN' ADVICE.

Oft hev Ah lang'd yon hill te clim',
Te hev a bit mair pross wiv him,
Wheeas coonsil, like a pleeasin' dreeam,
    Iz dear te me ;
Sen roond this warld sike chaps az him
      Seea few ther be.

Corruptin' beeaks he did detest,
Fer hiz wer ov the varra best,
This meead him wahzer ner all t' rist,
    O' t' nighbers roond ;
Thoff poor i' poss, wi' senses blist
      An' judgment soond.

Afooar the silver neet ov age,
The precepts ov the sacred page
Hiz meditashin did engage,
     That race te run ;
Like thooas weeah, spite o' Sattan's rage,
     The prahz hed won.

Bud noo hiz e'en 's geean dim i' deeath,
Neea mair a pilgram here on t' yeeath,
Hiz sowl flit fra' her shell beneeath,
    Te realms o' day ;
Whare carpin' care, an pain, an' deeath,
    Iz deean way.

Wivoot t' poor author's neeam or leeave,
Tha 've put hiz stooary thruff ther seeave,
An' roond hiz circuit set ther screeave
    O' justice keean ;
Fra' crotshits, cramps, an' simmibreeaves
    Te sift him cleean.

T' chaige 'at tha ageean him bring
Iz harpin' owwer mitch o' yah string,—
He triumphs like a lahtle king
    Owwer fashans gay :
He 's owwer relidjous !—that 's the thing
    Tha meean te say.

Bud still Awd Ahzaak tells hiz teeal,
Owwer monny a plissent hill an' deeal,
Will sumtahms inte citties steeal,
    Ner sahlent be
Tell bairns strahv how te lisp hiz theeam
    Across yon sea.

At oor last, bud lastin' interview,
Hiz fav'rite theeam he did renew,
Fra' which a paraphrase he drew,
    An' thus began,
Convarsin' clear wi' frinndship trew,
    Like man te man.

" Ah lahtle thowt, az weel thoo knaws,
Thoo tit t' pooblic wad expooas
Mah awd gray cooat, wi' all it's flaws,
    An' staff an' all ;
Fer want ov which fooks prood when awd
    Seea offens fall.

Ah varry leeatly gat a hint
Tha 'd put oor stooary inte prent,
An' copies all roond t' cuntry sent,
    Beeath left an' reet :
Bud, if 't wer deean wi' gud intent,
    Gud luck gan wi' 't.

Fer all Ah sed wer meant fer gud,
If it wer reetly ondersteead,
Te sum, neea doot, me langwish wad
    Seeam quite abrupt ;
We 're all alike ov flesh an' bleead
    An' harts corrupt.

Fooaks oft leeak mair at bleead an' breedin'
Then at t' soobject they are readin',
An' thus awd Prejediz is feedin',
    I' system narraw :
Fer want o' pains te crack t' hard beean,
    They oft miss t' marraw.

Men still, iv spite ov all oor coashin,
Hanker efter heegh promoshin,
Like Evan's pills, or Rowland's looashin,
    Sahn'd be t' king;
We 're seea inclahn'd te self-devooashin,
    That is t' thing.

T' nashin still seeams discontent,
We 've strang debates i' paileyment,
Petishins on petishins sent
    Ther, all implooarin';
An' sum i doonjin's deep lament,
    Whahl they are snooarin'!

An' still owwer t' land a cloud hings dull,
An' we ma' thrust, an' they may pool,
Wi' *Ayes* an' *Noes*, eeach paper 's full,
    Wi' applause an' lafter;
An' all the gud for poor John Bull
    'S te cum here-efter!

Still let us cawmly wait tell t' end,—
On God, an' nut on man, depend:
Oor nashin 's woond iz bad te mend—
    Ommest uncurable!
Hiz Izrael He will still defend
    Wiv kahndness durable.

Bud numbers strangely hev backslidden,
An' deean theease things 'at wer ferbidden,
An' caused Hiz feeace fer te be hidden
    Be ackshins fool,
Tell scare a ray ov howp iz left
    Te cheer yan's sowl.

The coonsil Ah wad recommend,
Iz all te strahve ther lives te mend,
An' persevere untel the end,
    I' wod an' deed;
An' thoas al nivver want a frinnd
    I' t' tahm o' need!

Bud Ah mun cut mah stooary shooat,
Or it may mak yer criticks spooat,
Oor soobject's ov owwer grave a sooat
    Te dwell upon;
Afooar ya spreead yer next repooat,
    Ah sall be geean.

Fer sahn we met an' paited last,
Ah finnd mah strength iz gahin' fast,
Like floors aneeath a Nor'-Eeast blast,
       Yance fresh an' gay;
Seea man iz doom'd te droop an' weeast,
       An' fade away.

Ah wad, afooar Ah tak me leeave,
Te all, me deein' coonsil give,
An' if the trewth they deea believe
       Or apprehend,—
That trewth, whahl Ah 've a day te live,
       Ah will defend."

Awd Abzaak's Deein' Advice.

When Eden's flowory gardin smahl'd,
Ner t' sarpint hed poor Eve begahl'd,
Man steead upreet an' undefahl'd
       I' mahnd an' feeater,
An' mutuwal conversashin held
       Wiv hiz Creator.

Bud when that deeadly monster, Sin,
Had yance gain'd an entrance in
Tit whahld, oor sorrows did begin,
       An' Heeaven froon'd,
An' t' glitt'ring swoord ov justice gleeam'd
       On all-aroond.

Sin spred destruckshin wahd, an' seean
Grim Deeath began hiz fearful reean,
Sattan wiv lees an' mallas keen
       Went teea an' fro',
All t' frail, thoff nowble, suns o' men
       Te owwerthraw.

Bud the Almighty sent Hiz aid,
Enoch an' Abraham obey'd,
An' Noah, an' Job, an' Daniel pray'd,
       An' Gideon teea;
An' mighty foes thruff mighty faith
       Tha did subdeea.

Then ancient Izrael's altars bleeaz'd,
An' sollem congregashins gaz'd,
An' holy men ther voices raiz'd,
    An' trumpits soonded;
Then heeathen aimies steead amaz'd,
    An' wer confoonded.

Then Joshua conker'd i' the deeal,
An' gud Elijah did preveeal,
The wicked wershippers o' Baal
    He owwerthrew,
An' show'd te them the livin' God,
    An' only trew.

Then whahl the sacrifice waz pure,
Destructshin com nut neegh ther dour;
I' moont er tent tha wer secure,
    Be neet er day,
Whahl thravin' groops o' flocks an' heeards
    All roond 'em lay.

Tha towt an' show'd ther childer hoo
Ther fayders kept ther sollem voo,
When the Almighty led 'em throo
    The dessot land;
An' hoo thooas fell 'at wad n't boo
    Te Hiz command.

An' seea sud we wer childer teeach,
An' in ther ears gud doctrin preeach,
Afooar corrupt idees can reeach
    Ther tender mahnd;
Te finnd when tha te manhud reeach,
    The gud disahn'd.

Ey, tell 'em wheea t' awd sarpant stang,
Hoo Moses towt an' Deborah sang,
An' hoo the holy Hebrews yung
    Did woke thruff fire;
An' try te teean ther infant tungs
    Te David's lyre.

Remahnd 'em ov a Saviour's luv,
Larn 'em the ways God will appruv,
Te pray an' fix ther thowts abuv
    Yeth's fleetin' joys;
Whilk at ther best when tried al preeav
    Bud empty toys.

Consult the warthies ov eeach age,
Wheeas lives are doon i' t' sacred page,
Ner rist tell all the hart engage
    Like them i' fight;
Then we like them oor hostile fooas
    Sall put te flight.

Tiv uz tha fer egzamples stand,
Lahk gahd-posts iv a weeary land,
Or lahk seea monny beeacons grand
    On mountains heegh,
Te show uz t' rooad Jehovah 'z plann'd,
    Er danger neegh.

Bud men graw noo seea wahldly wahz,
Seea prooan te vanitee an' lees,
The best o' coonsil tha 'll dispahz,
    Seea queer tha liv;
Tha 'll scarce a propper queston ax,
    Er anser giv.

Mankahnd i' general can spy
A mooat 'at 'z in annudder's e'e;
An' big an' bizzy az Paul Pry
    Te mark it doon;—
It helps fra' silly passers by
    Te felt ther awn.

Ther 's numbers seeams o' t' better sooat,
'At round our chapils will rezooat,
An' o' convershin mak a spooat,
    An' sins forgi'en;
An' at the trewly pious shut
    Ther arrows keen.

— Bud the Almighty seez ther ways,
An', thoff he lengthens oot ther days,
An' His just wrath He now delays,
    'T iz seer te cum;
The stootest o' the human race
    Mun meet ther doom.

Ey, when ther jolly days ar spent,
If tha deea nut i' tahm repent,
Tha 'll seerly doon te Hell be sent
    Te revil theer;
Te koss, an' foam, an' pay ther rint
    I' black dispair.

Freeat nut theesel' when thoo diz see
T' wicked iv hiz prosperitee,
Te florrish like a green bay tree,
 Er cedar tall ;
Tha like a leeaf, be firm decree,
 Mun fade an' fall.

Consider thoo what hez been sed,
An' o' ther threeats be nivver flay'd,
Beware lest thoo sud be betray'd,
 Be ther dissait ;
Gi'e t' Lord thee hart, an' deea n't dispahz,
 Hiz Sperrit 's leet.

  * * * *

T' cuntree seeams all anxiety
Te knaw Awd Ahzaak's pedigree,
An' sum rooar oot, —" *It's all a lee !*
 A meead up thing ! "
Te sike we think it nut worth whahl
 Wer preeafs te bring. ·

Fer all 'at wish te knaw, mah read
The sum an' soobstance ov hiz creed,—
Mah catch an' saw the lahtle seed,
 Wiv greeat success :
But whare he lived, an' whare he deed,
 Iz left te guess.

AWD AHZAAK'S STOOARY'S ENDID.

Tailpiece by Bewick.

T' LEEALHOLM CHAP'S LUCKY DREEAM,

OR, AN AWD THING RENEW'D.

Yah Kessenmas neet, or then aboot,
When meeasons all wor frozzen oot,
Ah went te see a cuntry frinnd,
An hospitubbel hoor te spinnd.
Fer gains Ah cut across o' t' moor,
Whoor t' snaw seea furosly did stour.
T' hoos Ah geeand, an' enter'd in,
An' wer az welcome az a king.
T' storm ageean t' awd winder patter'd,
An' t' hailsteeans doon t' chimler clatter'd;
All hands wer in, an' seeam'd content,
An' neean did frost er snaw lament.
T' lasses all wer at ther sewin',
Ther cheeaks wi' hilth an' beauty glowin'.
Aroond t' looa heearth, i' cheerful chat,
Tweea 'r three frinndly nighbers sat;
Ther travils tellin',—whare tha 'd been,
An' what tha hed beeath heeard an' seen;
Tell yan uz all did mitch amuse,
An' thus a stooary introduce.
  " Ah rickollect lang sahn," sez he,
" A stooary 'at wer telt te me,
'At seeams seea strange i' this oor day,
That trew or fause Ah cannut say.
  A man liv'd i' this nighberhud,
Neea doot ov reputashin gud,
An' lang tahm straahve, wi' stiddy care,
Te keep hiz hooshod i' repair.
At length he hed a curos dreeam,
(Fer three neets runnin' 't wer all t' seeam,)
'At if on Lunnon Brigg he stud,
He'd hear sum news wad deea him gud.

He laber'd hard, beeath neet an' day,
Tryin' te drahve thooas thowts away,
Bud daily grew mair discontent,
Tell he at last te Lunnon went.
Bein' quite a stranger te that toon,
Lang tahm he wanner'd oop an' doon,
Tell led biv sum mysterous hand,
On Lunnon Brigg he teeak hiz stand;
An' theer he waited day be day,
An' just wer boon te cum away,
Seea mitch he thowt he wer te bleeam,
Te gan' seea far aboot a dreeam,
When thus a chap, as he drew near,
Did ax, 'Good friend, what seek you here,
Where I have seen you soon and late?'
   Hiz dreeam tiv him he did relate.
'Dreams,' sez the man, 'are empty things,
Mere thoughts that flit on silver'd wings;
Unheeded we should let them pass,
I 've had a dream, and thus it was:
That somewhere round this peopled ball,
There 'z such a place as Lealholm Hall.
Yet whether such a place there be,
Or not, is all unknown to me.
There, 'neath a cellar dark and deep,
Where slimy creatures nightly creep,
And human footsteps never tread,
There is a store of treasure hid.
If it be so, I have no doubt
Some lucky wight will find it out:
Yet true or false is nought to me,
For I shall ne'er go there to see!'
   Oor Leealholm friend did twice er thrice
Thenk t' cockney chap fer hiz advice;
Then heeam ageean, withoot delay,
He cheerfully did tak hiz way.
   Settin' aboot hiz wark he sped—
Fund ivvery thing az t' man hed sed;
Wer ivvor efter seen te florrish,
T' fahnest gentleman i'.t' parish.
Fooaks wunner'd sair, an' weel tha meet,
Whare he gat all hiz ginnees breet!
   If it wer trew, i' spite o' fecam,
It wer te him a lucky dreeam!"

T' BEELDIN' O' GLAISDILL BRIGG.

A RUFF JOB FER BEEATH MAISTER AN' MEN IV 1828.

PAIT FOST.

WHERIVVER yan gans te tak a woak,
This brigg iz all the common toak;
Fer wedder it be leeat er seean,
Ther cry iz, " Har n't ya ommeast deean? "

A nighber sed te Matty Hall,
He thowt this brigg wad kill uz all:
Bud hoo this prophecee ma muv,
Seean tahm er Providence will pruv.

Bud seer t' experimental pait,
Wad ding a hero oot o' hairt,
When we reflect on what iz past,
An' gannin' on fra fost te last.

Geoorge Tinker com when t' job began,
Bud acted like a cunnin' man;
Fer t' hill wer owwer hard te clim,
An' seean the gam waz up wiv him.

Then Pritty com i' t' heat o' t' thrang,
An' prommist fair fer stoppin' lang;
Bud he be chance gat strange an' leeam,
An' we had him te carry heeam.

An' Silversahd hez left i' det,
An' Johnson 'z teean away i' t' pet;
Fletcher wad neea laugher stay,
An' Gibson sez he 'll run away.

Pearson toaks ov weary beeans,—
He 'z ommest kill'd wi' cuttin' steeans;
An' Castillo he 'z lang been seek,—
He seldom gits fahve days i' t' week.

An' Cruddaz cums nobbut now an' then,
An 'z reckont yan ov oor heead men;
An' Breckon, he 'z nut lang been wiv uz,
An' riddy onny day te leeav uz.

Oor maister 'z hed ruff rooad te pass,—
Tha 've straiten'd him fer want o' brass;
An' t' men wad hev ther wages raized,—
'T 'z aneeaf te set a maister craized.

Seca opposishin greeat an' small
Had dampt the sperrits ov uz all!
We fondly thowt oor trade wad florrish,
Suppooated be a wealthy parish.

Bud awkard fields, an' narrow riggs,
Tha 've spoilt uz quite fer beeldin' briggs;
Ner iz it common i' this nashin
Te beeld 'em on a dry foundashin.

Wiv all ther petty plans an' prices,
Tha teear a workman all te pieces;
An' if tha git ther ends aboot,
Oor meeasons seean ma worhk fer nowt.

Ther 'z yan 'at aims he 'z i' famus graith,—
He laffs an' maks a spooat o' faith;
A tahm ma cum, wiv visage grim,
When he ma wish hiz lamp te trim.

Noo sike a man sud fost be seen
Te git all t' sceeals teean off hiz een;
An' try te beeld a brigg at yance
Across t' wahd gulf ov ignorance.*

Annudder wheea disarves a stripe,
He 'z rayder reeasty iv hiz pipe,
He awluz had a deal te say,
Bud scarce a penny will he pay!

We hev sum condescendin' men,
Ther ma neea doot be yan i' ten,
That ken the legal tahm o' day,
An' help uz on withoot delay.

We 've yan 'at lens a helpin' hand
At yance possesst beeath hoos an' land;

The Inscription on the Bridge is, ' Ponder thy path, for genuine faith can build a bridge across the gulf of death.'

He 'z ommest eeghty year ov age,
He brings hiz meeat, an' taks neea wage !

Wiv furrow'd cheeaks an' hooary hairs,
He 'z gi'en uz monny faithful days ;
He leeaks thruff hardships, creeak'd an' coll'd,
Tiv hiz reward i' t' udder woll'd.

We hev annudder royal meeason,
That diz n't put annudder feeace on ;
Bud freely cums te help uz throo,
An' brings a lusty prentis too.

Had Wallis cum, wiv all his brags,
He might hev geean wiv empty bags,
Unless 'at 't parish jurisdickshin
Had meead it up be a soobscripshin.

May uz 'at 'z left, like trew-drawin' hosses,
Tak up wiv all oor rubs an' crosses ;
Fer efter al! this toil an' pain,
We howp 'at t' sun 'll shahn ageean !

Tailpiece by Bewick.

PAIT SECOND

Tha tell uz oft, when we 're away,
Bud meeastly ov a Sabbath day,
Oor brigg is crooded wiv inspecters,
'At rahze aboot it queer conjecters.

Sum grit men, wi' judishus sarch,
Hev spied a crack o' tweea i' t' arch,
An' sends t' alarm fra toon te toon
'At seer aneeaf 't 'll tummel doon.

Sumboddy raist a dreeadful teeal,
Hoo it hed freeten'd Jooasuff Deeal;
He com te see 't yah Sabbath day,
An' just leeakt up, an' ran away.

He thowt he heer'd sumboddy say,
Tha thowt tha seed it givin' way!
He ran seea fast that nowt cud tonn him,
For fear 'at t' brigg sud tummel on him.

It wor neea joke, fer far aboon,
He ommest ran a woman doon; *
An' if sheea owwer t' bows had geean,
He 'd kill'd er leeam'd her, ten te yan.

Bud efter all 'at 'z deean an' sed,
Ther iz neea cayshin te be flay'd:
Whahl t' prisent fahmers hods ther land,
Ther iz neea fear bud t' brigg 'll stand.

Bud ther iz sum unlucky lads
'At wants correctin' be ther dads;
Tha might be iv sum better pleeace
Ner thrawin' steeans 'at t' awd man's feeace.†

* Sheea wor readin' t' inscripshin'
† T' feeace on t' kyghsteean o' t' brigg wer damisht wi' t' 'ads thrawin'
steeans at it.

PICKERIN' STEEPLE CHASS.

JOE.

WEEL, Jim, hoo deea lad? What iz t' news?
What sahd is thoo on?—Pinks er Blews?
Here 'z sike a mighty stir i' t' nashin,
It 'z worth a lahtle conversashin.
Ah want te knaw, iz 't reet er wrang?
Unless thah narves iz varra strang,
Ah hev a paper i' me pockit
'Ll lift the hart oot ov its sockit!

JIM.

A paper, Joe! what iz 't aboot?
Sum monney matter tha 'z neea doot!
Sum Mettody er Ranter bodder,
Er sum Teetotal thing er udder.
Yan scarce can pass alang a street,
Bud sum sike like yan 'z seer te meet,
Wheea 'd ommest sweer 'at black iz white,
Te gain annudder prosselite.

JOE.

A monney matter 't iz ov cooas,
Fra quite an opposisshin sooas,
Fer, be tha Liverpool Recooader,
'T iz mair like ov t' Succeshin Ooader;
Althoff 't iz sed, be snug repooat,
Religious fooak hev gi'en 't suppooat.
That 'at Ah noo te nooatis bring
Iz t' Steeple Chass at Pickerin'.

JIM.

Whyah, Joe, thoo 'z neean o' t' warst o' fellaz,
Seea squat tha doon a bit an' tell uz,
If thoo sud think it neea disgrass,
Aboot thiz meeghty Steeple Chass;—
Ov hoo, an' when, an' whare tha run,
Fer honnor, monney, er fer fun.

Thoo 'z just gi'en ma an itchin' ear,—
It 'z t' varra thing Ah wish te hear.

JOE.
Thoo seez, upon a sartin day,
Ah hennut seen, bud heeard 'em say,
Grit gentilmen hev hosses train'd,
Fia lofty pedigree obtain'd,
Seea full o' bleead, an' queerly towt,
Te gallop thruff er owwer owt.
All muster at a sartin pleeace,
An' this tha call ther Steeple Chass.
A poss o' gowld tha then prisent,
An' wod iz thruff all t' cuntrey sent.
Fer fowwer mahl, Ah think, tha run,
An' he 'at beeats, the steeaks 'z hiz awn.
Sum breeak ther necks wi' missin' bridges,
An' sum gits stuck wi' jumpin' hedges !
Ay, te confirm 'at trewth Ah sing,
Tha kilt a hoss at Pickerin'.

JIM.
Whyah, Joe ! thoo quite supprahzes me,
Te think 'at men ov heegh degree
Sud reallie hev neea mair rispecks
Fer nowder t' men ner t' hosses' necks.

JOE.
A hoss iz nowt i' sike a keease !
Bairn, sowls iz nowt at t' Steeple Chass !
Tha fer a trifle swap an' sell 'em ;
An' t' pahsons hez n't sense te tell 'em
That t' Steeple Chass iz suited quite
Te glut ther carnal appetite.
Thooas 'at ther Bahbles luv an' preear,
'Ll finnd bud bareish pickin' theer.

JIM.
Mahnd, Joe, thoo iz n't owwer severe,
An' 'at thah coonsil be sincere ;
Fer t' law hez monny kuros links,—
Man mooant speeak awluz az he thinks.
Thoff Ah mesel' feel shockt te think
Men sud seea push te ruin's brink,
Mitch mair te be inkorridged in
What mun be a presumpteous sin.

JOE.

Man, mair Ah see this standart reeazt,
An' mair an' mair Ah stand ameeazt,
Te think 'at pahsons sud n't see 't,
An' tell 'em plain it iz n't reet:
'At men sike docktrin sud procleeam,
An' thooas 'at beer t' Christian neeam,
I' spite ov all divine advice,
Sud sankshin sike a sweepin' vice.

JIM.

Whativver be ther settisfackshin,
It hez a wonnerful attrackshin,
An' maks 'em freely stir ther shanks,
'Specially them o' t' heegher ranks.
Frev Scarbro', Malton, York, an' Leeds,
Tha cum on lofty-moonted steeds,
Owwer dazzelin' ommost te behowl'd,
Wiv silvert whips an' cheeans o' gowld.
Theer 'z bans o' music, cullers fleein',
Hams an' legs o' mutton freyin';
Nimmel waiters upon t' wing
Te sell 'em drink an' hear 'em sing;
Theer 'z gammelin' teeabels, orringe stalls,
Spice, an' nuts, an' dancin' dolls:
All things te suit ther carnal teeast
May just be fund at t' Steeple Chass.

JOE.

Thooas men hev getten 't i' ther poower
Carin' nowt fer t' starvin' poor,
Te gallop owwer hedge an' dyke,
An' deea an' say just what tha like;
An' all t' tahm tha run thooas rigs,
An' sing, an' drink, an' dance ther jigs,
They 'll booast ov nowbel ancestry,
An' meeghty steeple pedigree.
If onny wish tha cause te knaw,
Hoo tha are yabbel te deea so,
" 'T iz monney maks the meer te gang,"
Maks wrang seeam reet an' reet seeam wrang.

JIM.

Bud t' thing sud be te them meead knawn,
'At t' gowld an' silver 'z nut ther awn;
'At t' cattle tha abuse an' kill

Belangs tiv t' Lord o' Zion's hill.
Tha sud be wahn'd i' ivvery pleeace
Te giv up all sike wickid ways ;
Er seer az ther 'z a God aboon,
Tha 'll pool ther awn destruckshin doon.

JOE.

Tha hev been wahn'd, an' hev refused,
Whahl thooas gud things tha hev abused ;
Be which abuse tha breeak God's law,
An' that He 'll sum day let 'em knaw.
This maks 'em breeathe pernishous breeath,
An' swagger on tit varge o' deeath ;
Whahl udders, rayder then controwl,
'Ll breeak ther necks, an' loss ther sowl.

JIM.

A chap telt me, be way o' crack,
Bud kahnd o' trimmel'd az he spak,
Tha 'd docters pleeact, wivin a shoot,
Te slip necks in 'at gat slipt oot. *

JOE.

It 'z awful booastin' this indeed,—
Bad sample ov beeath fruit an' seed !
Sike ma upbraid the warld wi' sizm,
This iz next dooher te soshalizm.
Sike booastin' tha will sum day rue,
If we admit wer Bahbel trew.
All thooas mun pass a meeghty change
Afooar on t' happy hills tha range.
Bud tiv oor teeal—let uz tonn back,
Lest wa git farder frev oor track.
T' greeat day arrahves, an' t' smahlin' sun
Proclaims ther Steeple Chass begun.
On eeager lugs then t' tumult steeals,
Ov prancin' steeds an' rummellin' wheels.
It wer a day ov winks an' nods,
Ov lofty deeds an' lofty wods ;
Az thoff tha hed fer ther defense
All t' thunner ov Omnipotence.
Then fooaks com rowlin' in be skooars,
Frev nighb'rin' toons, an' off o' t' mooars ;
Like cloods o' locusts in tha hale,
Fra Gooadland, Sleights, an' Harwood-deeal.

* Yan o' ther fost-rate rahders sed 'at he carried a lowse neck iv his
pockit, i' keeas owt happent hiz awn.

'T iz seerlie sum inchantit string .
'At diz sike croods tegidder bring.
Like beez tha roond ther Steeple swarm,
Iv that tha lahklee see neea hahm.

JIM.

Neea hahm !—what hahm, Joe, can ther be
Iv seein' sike a raritee
Ov men an' hosses heeghly feead,
Wi' preeasts an' squires at ther heead ?
Ov gentilmen an' ladies gay,
Az bonny az the flowers o' May ?
Thare riches, yuth, an' beauty shahn,
Array'd i' silk an' superfahn.
An' fahmer maidens, yung an' fair,
Yan wonners hoo tha 've tahm te spare ;
Wi' lads o' manners ruff an' rude,
All mixin' i' yah multitude.
An' poor awd men 'at scarce can blaw,
Wi' beeards an' whiskers white az snaw ;
Sad sample ov oor fallen race,
All rollin' up tit Steeple Chass.
An' fahmer sarvants leeave ther plew,
Callin' ther maisters black an' blew,
Wheeah fer ther creedit an' gud neeam
Hed coonsilt 'em te stop at heeam.
Ah met 'em az Ah com alang,
(Tha wonnert whyah Ah wad n't gang)
Wi' rooasy cheeaks an' shooders breead,
Bettin' wagers upon t' rooad.
Ther leeaks an' wods at yance declare
Ther trizher an' ther harts iz theer.
If yah contrary sentence drop,
That mouth at yance tha try te stop.
Bud when roond t' splendid stand tha meet,
'T wad deea a blinnd man gud te see 't !
Besahdes thooaz men 'z seea fahnly drisst
A Steeple Chass! whyah weeah wad miss 't?

JOE.

Frev fost te last, it iz desahn'd
Te pleease, te fascinate the mahnd ;
Te lift it, az on eeagil's wings,
An' drahve off thowts ov better things.
T' stewhads, full o' warldly wit,

Pronounce 'at all things noo ar fit,
When thoosans then rowl'd up te see,
Az drawn be steeple witchery.
Ther 'z joiners, meeasons, bricklays, carters,
Careless o' ther futer quarters,
Leeave the scaffold, rooad, er shop,
Ner waits te lap ther happrons up;
All i' sike a mighty strather,
Fit te treead o' yan annudder.
Mudders careless o' ther sun,
Callin' t' bairns 'at weea n't cum on.
Fra whence tha cum, er whoor tha dwell,
If yoo 've a paper it 'll tell.
You ken the hosses wheeas tha ar
Be t' cullers 'at ther rahders weear.
Thus wedder i' the rooad er no,
Wi' whip an' spoor, away tha goa!
Owwer hedge an' dyke, ther's nowt can stop'm,
Unless an angry God unprop 'em.
Thus rahdin' owwer gess er kooan
'At 'z growin' er 'at 'z leeatly sawn,
Thare 'z neean dahr lift a hand, er say,
"What hev ya deean?" er "Wheea'z te pay?"
Whahl oaths profane an' lafter lood
Ar utter'd be the geeapin' crood:—
Be sum wheea yance religion luv'd,—
Nut nobbut sangshinn'd, bud appruv'd,
If ivvery wod an' seeacrit thowt
Mun yah day be te judgment browt,
O, hoo unlike sike wark az this
Iz that 'at leads te gloaryas bliss!
Te see 'em all seea blahth an' merry
Waz famus pastahm fer Awd Herry!
If owt te him cud be deleeghtin',
'T wad be te see 'em drunk an' feeghtin'.
He popt aboot amang the people,
At last he popt up on tit steeple,
Oppen'd a pair ov dizmal jaws,
Flapt hiz black wings, an' yawn'd applause.
Like sum prood emperor ov awd,
Upon the weddercock he rade;
Whoor he mud all at yance sorvay
The grand proceedins ov that day.
A flag-staff fer a whip he seeaz'd,

An' spoort the spire, he wor seea pleeaz'd
Te think it sud hiz cause diffend,
An' that hiz bait hed ansert t' end.

JIM.

It 'z nut fer thoo te critesahz
On men seea greeat, seea rich, seea wahz.
Tha aim, neea doot, az weel az thee,
Te gan' te Heeaven when tha dee.
What, thoff ther munney be bud lent,
Thoo knaws 'at munney mun be spent:
Besahdes, tha hev example teea,—
If t' *pahson* 'z theer, what 'z that te theea?

JOE.

If thooas sud miss ther passidge heeam,
A careless priesthud tha ma bleeam;
Blinnd guides tha ar, an' t' kirk'z ther mudder,
An' tha weea n't gang te hear annudder.
We Christians run a diff'rent race,
Te what ya call yer Steeple Chass;
Besahdes, we finnd i' Holy Writ,
Ther 'z neean cums theer 'at ar nut fit.

JIM.

Thoo means te preev be argiment,
Thooas 'at cum theer mun fost repent,
An' be thruff Jesus Christ fergiven
Afooar tha 're i' the rooad te Heeaven.
Neea carnal plizher tha mun share,
Bud liv a life ov faith an' pray'r.
If thooaz aleean hev savin' grace,
Doon gans at yance the Steeple Chass!

JOE.

Seea lejins fell frev leet te dark,—
Seea Dagon fell afooar the ark,—
Seea God prood Pharoah owwerthrew,
Wiv Sisera, an' Goliah teea,—
Seea fell the lords i' sad serprahz
Wheeaz hands hed put oot Samson's eyes.
Thooaz meeghty men wer tonn'd te dust,—
An' seean thooaz Steeple Chassers must.
Whyah, Joe, it cap ma fair te ken,
Hoo thooaz heegh-fleeing' gentilmen
Can, frev ther chassin' gan te t' kirk,

An' join i' t' blissid Sunda's wark,
Singin' wiv all ther meeght an' main,
This Heeaven-inspired, this holy strain :—
" Let all thy converse be sincere,
Thy conscience as the noon-day clear ;
For God's all-seeing eye surveys
Thy secret thoughts, thy words and ways."
An' then frev t' kirk tit Steeple Chass,
An' set at nowt God's luv an' grace,
Call t' dissenters all thruff t' nashin
Fer *Apostolical Successhin !*

JOE.

Te bring oor soobject tiv a clooas,—
Oor aim is nobbut te expooas
The thing Almighty God diz hate—
Nut te provooak unkahnd debate.
The day 'z nut far 'at will reveeal
The trewth, an' fix the final seeal.
Sum ma, when it 'z owwer leeat te rew,
Finnd what tha howp'd wer fause, iz trew,
Consarnin' ivverlastin' woe !

Tailpiece by Bewick.

D

POOHER PATCH.

Pooher Patch waz browt up tit scratch,
 An' markt oot fer bein' a glutton;
  Wiv hiz neck iv a string,
  He wer sentenced te swing,
 'Koas he'd grown sike a laddie fer mutton.

A bit ov a leg he happent te beg,
 Az doon Jack-sled-gate he wer trudgin';
  Be carryin' on 't heeam,
  He gat all the bleeam,
 An' he wer te be hang'd wivoot judgin'.

He seeam'd fer te say, at the clooas o' t' day
 Te t' dogs 'at he happent te see:—
  "Tak warnin' be me,
  When yer oot on the spree,
 Er ya 'll hing on a gallas az heegh!

Ther'z monny mair left 'at ar laddies fer theft,
 A vast mair fer takkin' then givin';
  Sheep 'll be worried,
  Thoff Ah 'm seea hurry'd
 Away frev tha land o' the livin'."

Tailpiece by Linton.

ROOASDILL BOB AN' HARTOFT JOHN.

JOHN.

WHAT cheer, awd stock?—say what'z ther been te doo,
'At maks ya leeak seea dark aboot yer broo?
Ya leeak az thoff yer parleyment petishin,
Hed met wi' sum rooamantic opposisshin.
Er mebby yoo hev met wi' sum abuse,
Er frev sum quahter heeard sum hevvy news.
Mebby the trial ma cum clooaser still,
Yer wahf er childer ma be takken ill.

BOB.

Alas! the news Ah hev te tell 'z seea bad
'At t' feeldz an' forrists seeam i' monnin' clad!
Be men unawthorahz'd an' unahdeean'd
Oor new-erictet temple iz profeean'd.
Tho cushins an' the tasshils all ar soilt,
The bell 'z inchantit, an' oor warshop 'z spoilt.
Tha 've held iv it—what 'z cawzt this desecrayshin?—
A meetin' fer the Bahbel's sirkalayshin!

JOHN.

If that be all, whyah t' thing 'z az leet az kaff!
The feeldz an' fleeads ma clap ther hans an' laff;
Sen' better sense iz teeachin' greeat an' small
Te send Hiz gloryez leet fra powl te powl.
'T iz yan o' Jesus Christ's last greeat commands
Te send this leet te dark an' heeathen lands.
Let 'z howp the profit 'll ootweygh the loss;
If t' parson beea n't, whyah t' chetch 'll be neea warse.

BOB.

Whyah, Ah 'z neea scholard, nowder will pertend
Te say hoo far this mischief ma extend.
Oor greeat Divahn, afooar He left the pleeace,
He telt uz posativ it wer the kecas:

D 2

Hiz argiment did rahz te that amoont,
The chetch wer ruint on this seeam account.
When sike like wark the chetch's pillahs shak,
Hiz Maister's honner fooast him fer te speeak.

JOHN.

Wedder Divahn, M.A., er LL.D.,
T' iz lahtel matter wheea er what he be;
Fer t' thing 'z reveealt tiv uz az weel az him,—
What God appreeavs, man owt nut te condemn.
Whativver ma be hiz sahserdooatal geeans,
Whyah t' pooblic ma weel thenk him fer hiz peeans,
'At he seea fahn a sampel sud dispense
Ov collidge-eddicated impedense.

BOB.

Kud it be heeard an' ondersteead areet,
Daft Hannah's speeach wad be quite full o' leet.
Sheea thinks t' awd man sud nut ha' been seea vext,
Bud tónn'd hiz leeaf, an' teean annudder text.
All t' bad iffecks hez bin, sheea hez neea doot,
Wi' brush an' beezom, swept an' carried oot:
Tha teeak trew pains te mak all clean an' chivver,
An' t' chetch iz noo az gud an' weel az ivver.

JOHN.

Bud leeaks thoo heer, this iz the thing tha dreead,—
If yance tho Bahbel an' the trewth we spreead,
The veil 'll fall fra off the peepel's e'es,
An' t' commons then will az ther lords be wahz;
Tha then 'll graw seea bowld i' disposhisshin,
Te heegher poohers tha will disdain submisshin;
An' will, te men ov honerubbel neeam,
Refuse that hommidge 'at ther titles claim !

BOB.

Then chapils will iv all dereckshins rahz,
Wiv saucy steepels moontin' te the skaihs;
An' preeachers run, er rahd wiv hoss er gig,
Az rank az sheep 'at travil Blaky Rigg.
If sike prosseedins fodder be allood,
Awd Inglin's sun 'll set behint a clood;
Ner sud wa wunner tha alood procleeam,
Thooas men sal speeak neea langher iv His neeam.

JOHN.

'At sike a meetin' sud be held i' t' chetch,

Be men 'at scarse wer fit te stan' i' t' pooatch,
Wer sike an a stain upon itz consecrayshin
Az roozt his riverence's indignayshin.
Fer what cud thooaz expect az ther reward,
Bud frev sike bowld attimpts te be debarr'd ? ·
Noo nivver mair mun tha cum theer ageean,
Whahl he hiz sacrid office diz susteean.
If sike like doctrins spreead an' sud prevail,
Then bishop's ordinayshin treead 'll fail ;
Then grace 'll mair then larnin' be admired,
An' preeasts stan' i' the markit-pleeace onhired ;
Men will frev ivvery seeacrit kooaner creeap,
An' oot o' kooalpits in tit poolpit leeap ;
Whahl wi' ther jesters an' ther insinewayshins
Tha 'll rob t' awd chetches o' ther congregayshins.

BOB.

Then fooaks 'll tonn, lahk beez 'at 'z left ther hahv,
Seea stupid 'at tha 'll nowder leead ner drahv,
Ner draw be gifts, ner binnd doon be oppresshin,
Ner scar be Apostolecal Suckshesshin.
I' vain a man ma then hiz feeace dizgahz,
An' lanlords owwer ther tenants tyrannahz.
Neea patchwark then 'll anser az afooar,
Ner goons, ner blankits buy er sell the pooher.
That parson then ma chance te loss hiz pleeace
Wheea hunts, er gallops i' a Steepel Chass ;
Wheea i' the ring appears a jovial fella,
Sits be hiz wahn er grog tell he iz mella ;
Wheea wiv hiz dogs persews the grooz er gam,
Mair then the cottidge o' the pooher er leeam ;
Er, if hiz gun sud chance te miss her mark,
Will rap an' sweear, an' lie all t' blecam on t' clark.

JOHN.

Deea n't wunner thoo 'at t' vinerubbel man
Sud be seea feearful ov hiz treead an' clan ;
If better leet wa spreead owwer lan' an' sea,
Oor heeam-bun slaves 'll seeak fer liberty.
Tha 'll finnd ther 'z neean seea fit te show the way
Az thooaz 'at woaks therein beeath neet an' day.
But God Hizsel' hez teean the thing i' hand,
An' Bahbel meetins yit 'll bliss the land.
Oor God 'll rahz up men ov nowbel sowl,
An' He the sleepy chetches will controwl ;

Will send Hiz sahvants, wheea His judgments knaw,
Te thunner oot the terrors ov Hiz law ;
Whahl Jesus will Hiz meeghty ame mak bare,
An' tak the flocks Hizsel' intiv Hiz care.

Bob.

Sike laws amang oor heegh-up chaps exist
Az layberin' men finnd hard fer te resist.
O' t' Sabbath days tha rob beeath God an' man,—
That scrahb ma preeav this statement fause 'at can.
All hans mun hurrey seean az tha heer t' bell,
Tit steepel-hooz, lit t' preeast be what he will ;
An' thooaz 'at iz n't settisfied wi' t' kirk,
Mun owder quit ther fahm er loss ther wark.

John.

Thooaz laws mitch differ fra tha laws ov Heeaven,
Fra God te man fer hooally parpos given ;
Peeace te promooat, an' poot an' end te strife,
Te regilate hiz hooshod an' hiz life.
Iv hooally days, afooar the chetches fell,
Neea music soonded lahk the sabbath bell.
The ministers wer thowtful, hooally men,
Ner threeats wer needed, ner kumpulshin then.

Bob.

Yan wad be fain sike days ageean te see,
An' hear fooaks sing wi' luv an' melody,
Az yan hez read i' beeaks ov hooally men,
'At nowder kared fer fire ner lion's den ;
Bud dreeaded sin wi' all itz scorpion stings,
Mair ner the wrawth ov heeathen preeasts an' kings.
All wheea te God i' meek submisshin boo,
Thoff t' rooad be dark, He 'll awluz bring 'em throo.

John.

Jist wait a whahl, tell Tahm revarse the scene,
An' Anti-Christ hez hed hiz pumpos reean ;
When Parsekushin, wiv her tooach an' fark,
Sets carnal men an' ministers te wark,
Te help the Beeast te mak hiz proselites,
Te purge hiz fleear, an' bon the hypocrites,
Then thooaz wheea live an' hev the trewth maintain'd,
I' clearer leet 'll hev the thing egsplain'd.

WESLEYANISM AT EEASBY,

I' STOWSLA SIRKIT.

THA 're wakken'd at Eeasby! the Lord iz amang 'em,
Thoff tonn'd oot o' t' temple 'at youst te belang 'em;
Annudder we howp afooar lang 'll be beelt,
Whoor sinners thruff Christ ma hev pardin fer guilt. —
T' Lord seeams te oppen a way oot afooar 'em,
Thoff nighberin' lions hev aim'd te devoor 'em,
When t' awd maister mariner failt at the helm,
Tha thowt it wad all the consarn owwerwhelm;
An' when tha appear'd ov all succour bereft,
Tha endeeavour'd te freeten t' few 'at wer left.
Bud the Lord wer detarmin'd te be ther proteckshin, —
Te send 'em suppooat, an' gi'e 'em dereckshin;
If nobbut, like monney, tha wad n't betray Him,
Bud stick te that text, beeath te luv an' obey Him.
  Tha can't be content wi' ther steeple opinions,
Bud tha mun mak inrooads on udder's dominions;
Thoff theer's be i' gen'ral the fat an' the wilthy,
Fer t' want o' gud physic, tha seldom ar hilthy.
Hoo strange 'at tha sud sike fair temples erect,
Te modder the sowls in ther swooan te protect!
Bud strangher tha 'll fiund it o' you sahd the fleead,
Wi' ther hands an' ther garmints all stain'd i' ther bleead.
We need n't te wunder tha mak sike a fuss,—
Ther craft is i' danger fra rebels like uz:
Fer God can mak preeachers—hoo fearful the thowt—
Fra cobblers, er meeasons, er blacksmiths, er owt!
O yis! Doctor Pusey ma whet hiz awd grunders,
An' put on hiz captivz ther fetters an' blinnders;
Ther 'z pooher men iv Eeasby 'at ken hiz awd sang,
An' see the defect ov beeath him an' hiz gang.
He may scare 'em wi' taxes, wi' rates, an' oppresshin,
All thooaz wheea 're oot o' the lahn o' Successhin;
Thoff te preeav he 'z in 't, he 'z a varry poor chance,
Unless he gans owwer te t' Romans at yance.

Then t' Romans wad help him, an' think it all reet,
Te modder Dissenters, an' poot oot ther leet;
Te cut 'em i' pieces, te butcher an' bon 'em,—
Bud tell that iz the keeas, tha can't owwerton 'em.
Ner Stowsla, ner Yatton, ther frinnds will invite,
Ner Skelton, ner Brotton, ther effots unite ;
Tha 'll finnd, te ther mottificashin an' pain,
Tha hev fowt wi' t' winnd, an' hev layber'd i' vain.

POPERY.

POPERY iz what it waz, an' iz lahkly te be !
We 've hed a few sampels on 't owwer t' sea :
That when 'i ther pooher, on a sudden tha 'll tak ya,
An' if ya deea n't render submisshin, tha 'll mak ya.
Then, Prodistans, what will ya think o' yer suns,
Te see 'em be Friars, yer dowtcrs all Nuns ?
When the Pope ligs hiz han' on t' chetch an' t' peepel,
Wiv lahtel steean crosses neegh ivvery steepel,
I' vain will the sleepers then seeak fer redress,—
The meeghty invenshin iz seear o' success.
When yance Parsekushin leets up her awd smiddy,
(Fer monny ar better hawf Roman awlriddy)
Tha 'll darken ther dayleet 'at thus kondesends,
An' bon all ther Bahbels, te mak 'em amends !
It hez bin diskuvver'd, but offens owwer leeat,
An enimy's kisses ar full o' desait.
Then, warrihers, be wakken !—ther'z thoosans asleep ;
T' awd enimy iz soobtel, an' numeres, an' deep.
Then pray mitch, an' think mitch, yer Bahbels attind,
Whilk, next tiv itz Awthor, will preeav yer best frinnd.
An' dinnot be freeten'd !—yer Maister iz strang !
Jist deea az He bids ya, an' ya 'll nut git far wrang :
A bowshot ma leet iv the harness atweean,
If He guide the arrow—Jehovah Ah meean.

T' RACE COOARS I' RUINS.

THOWTS GETHER'D ON T' SPOT.

Neegh fotty years hev wing'd ther fleet,
Sahn heer we met wi' fond deleet,
When days wer fahn, an' hilth shooan breet,
 Te see the race,—
An' fondly fancied all wer reet,
 An' neea disgrace!

All ages frev the countree roond
Wer iv that livin' sahkel fund,
Az seean az tha hed heeard the soond
 Seea fain te see
T' stall o' spice spred upon t' grund,
 An' hev a spree.

Awd Memmy, on her profits bent,
Her barrils an' her bottles sent,
An' lusty men ther sarvice lent,
 An' maidens fair,
Te fix her steeaks an' pitch her tent,
 Er waiters theer.

Seean manners vulgar an' refahn'd,
Was i' yah hummel-jummel join'd,
An' sum wheea seeam'd az brudders kahnd,
 Afooar 't wer neet
Waz wiv her awd Jameeaca lahn'd,
 An' stript te feeght.

Ther winnin' post waz rahzed up,
An' t' ginnees inte t' pot wer poot;
(T' races wer beeath fer hoss an' feeat)
 Seea prood that day,
We seean beheld the champions strut
 An' clear ther way.

Ah saw fer yan, an' saw weel pleeast,
The tumult an' the crood increeast,

Whahl eeach the eeager moment seeazt,
            Te hev ther fill;
An' few wer wiv the questen teeazt,
            " Waz 't gud er ill ? "

Then men gav uz te drink ther yall—
Tha sad 't wad mak oor hair te coll,
An' help uz Fotton's wheel te whohl,
            An' win a prahze;
Bud sahn, we fund tha yan an' all
            Hed telt us lees !

Awd men wer theer, wi' nuts an' spice,
An' wimmen fierce wi' box an' dice,
An' udder gams ov heegher price:
            'T waz all ther cry,—
Cum, lads an' lasses, deea n't be nice!
            Cum, toss er buy !

Fra Runsick tha hed cum, an' Steers,
Wi' apples, orringes, an' peehers,
Wi' crabs an' lobsters i' ther geers,
            Fresh oot o' t' seas ;
An' buyers buzz'd aboot ther ears,
            Lahk swarms o' bees.

The swains wer trimm'd up i' ther best,
The maidens sum i' white wer drisst,
W' silken sashes roond the weeast,
            Seea meeghty fahn,
That sum wer led beyond the test
            Ov prudence lahn.

Heer gowld leeact hats an' silver cups
Hev glittert upon t' lang powl tops,
Whilk sarvt fer winndin' stops, an' props
            Te hod up t' riggin',
Whahl onderneeath ther smeeaky props
            The lads wer swiggin'.

Heer hez the jockey crackt hiz whip,
Callt fer hiz grog, an' gi'en 'em t' slip,
Just teean 'em in az nice az nip,
            Be sleeght ov hand,—
Then callt hiz hoss a base awd rip,
            'At wad n't stand !

Awd Memmy, wiv her R—'s an' G—'s,
Appeart az queen amang the bees,

Yit hed te mahnd her Q—'s an' P—'s,
    Te keep all reet,—
Te call the yungsters be degrees
    Te t' dance at neet.

Whahl tipsy luvers went off linkt,
Iv her awd pooch ther money chinkt;
Sheea tiv her tristy sarvant winkt,
    Seea full o' glee;
Then on the modist maiden blinkt
    Wi' t' udder e'e.

Prood sat sheea on her lahtel hill,
The bumper er the glass te fill,
An' poot the yungsters thruff the drill
    Ov dice er kade;
Her fahn-formt limbs hev lang ligg'd still
    I' yon chetchyade!

Her coffin tire hez geean te rust,
T' yance livin' form hez tonn'd te dust;
Seea if the warld bahd, we seean must
    All lig beneeath,
An' wait wer fahnal sentence just
    Ov life er deeath.

Bud few frev sike a pleeace er state
Wad lahk te share poor H——son's fate,
Er hev ther doonfall thus te date
    Amang the deead,—
Afooar he reacht hiz pastur gate
    Hiz sperrit fleead.

That crood, alas! whare ar tha noo?
Sum lahk the gess hev hed te boo,—
The lygh o' Deeath hez ligg'd 'em law;
    Tha 've hed ther day;
Udders, wheea hev iskeeapt his blaw,
    Ar growin' gray.

Heer solitude an' sahlance reign,
An' t' ling graws lang upon the plain,
Then scampert be beeath nymph an' swain,
    The spooats te see:
Sum furlooan sandy heeaps remain
    Whare t' youzt te be!

All ages, sexes, heegh an' law,
That crood hez meltit off lahk snaw;

An' sum, alas! fer owt we knaw,
    'At then steead viewin',
Fra sike things, iv etarnal woe,
    Ma trace ther ruin!

Sum few hev meead attempts ov leeat
The former days te imitate,
An' rahz thersels te heegher state
    Wi' warldly ointment;
Bud better leet hez markt ther fate
    Wi' disappointment.

Thooaz few remarks deea show uz clear
The quick decay ov all things heer,
An' speeak lood wods i' ivvery ear
    Ov meanin' vast,—
Sike nobbut az obtain God's fear
    Ther joy shall last.

Heer ma we larn a lesson greeat,
The wahz an' gud te immitate,—
Be udder's folly shun ther fate,
    An' count the cost,—
Leeast we repent when it 'z owwer leeat,
    An' all iz lost.

Fer Jesus offers noo Hiz grace
Te all oor wretched hewman race,
Te better ther depraved keeas,
    An' liv te Him,—
Te breeten up eeach gloomy feeace,
    An' vision dim.

Hiz sperrit will Hiz leet affod
Te show the majesty ov God,
An' t' rooad be all Hiz sahvants trod,
    An' marcy fiee,
Te all wheea sarch Hiz blissid wod,
    An' wish te see.

Wheea tonn ther feeat intiv Hiz ways,
The willin' soobjecks ov Hiz grace,
When tha hev run ther Christian race,
    Wiv Him sall be,—
Secure wivin Hiz hooally pleeace
    Hiz glooary see.

He calls Hiz weary wand'rers heeam,
An' censhers thooase wheea winnot cum,

An' threeatens wiv a fearsome doom
  All wheea rebel,—
That sike mun feel the wrath te cum
  An' fire ov Hell !

Ma we ferseeak oor wickid deeds,
An' melt whahl still Hiz marcy pleeads,
Giv up all fause an' fermal creeds
  Hiz wod condemns,—
Be fund, when He te judge uz cums,
  Amang Hiz gems !

Tailpiece by Bewick.

GLOSSARY.

(Abridged from "The People's History of Cleveland and its Vicinage," by George Markham Tweddell, *now publishing in 32 parts at 6d. each, or by Bookpost 7d., supplied to Subscribers only.)*

Aboon, above; common in the old English and Scottish ballads, and too fine a word to be allowed to die out. *Aboot,* or *abowt,* about. *Abuv,* above; a more modern word in the Dialect than aboon. *Ackshins,* actions. *Afeeat,* afoot, on foot. *Affod,* afford. *Afooar,* before; in its more polished form, *afore,* commonly used by the Elizabethan writers; Ben Jonson, for instance, was partial to it. *Afooar 't,* before it. *Afooar t',* before the. *Ageean,* again, or against. *Ah,* I. *Ah'd,* I had. *Ah'll,* I will. *Ah'm,* I am. *Ah s',* I shall. *Ah've,* I have. *Ah'z,* I am. *Ahzaak,* Isaac. *Aimies,* armies. *Al,* or *'ll,* will. *Alang,* along. *Aleean,* and *alooan,* alone. *Allood,* allowed. *All t',* all the. *Althoff,* although. *Amang,* among, and amongst; Chaucer's *emang* and *omang. Ame,* arm. *Ameeaz'd* and *ameeazt,* amazed. *Amoont,* amount. *An',* and. *An 'z,* and is, or and have. *An* is often used unnecessarily in the Dialect; as, for instance, "sike *an* a leeak oot," for such a look out. *Angils,* angels. *An' 't,* and it. *An' t',* and the. *An' 't 's,* and it is. *Aneeaf,* enough. *Aneeath,* beneath. *Annudder,* or *annuther,* another. *Annudder's,* or *annuther's,* belonging to another. *Anser,* answer. *Anserd,* answered. *Ansers,* answers. *Appeart,* appeared. *Appreav,* or *appruv,* approve; the latter being rather a provincial pronunciation than true Dialect. *Appreav'd,* or *appruv'd,* approved. *Appreaves,* approves. *Ar,* are. *Areet,* aright. *Argiment,* argument. *Aroond,* around, round about, encircling. *Arrahves,* arrives. *'At,* that. *'At 'z,* that is, that are, or that have. *Attimps,* attempts. *Attindid,* attended. *Attrackshin,* attraction. *Awd,* old. *Awn,* own: Tyndale, in both his translations of the New Testament (1525-6 and 1534) uses the word. *Awkard,* awkward, clumsy, unfavourable, unaccommodating. *Awlriddy,* already. *Awlus,* always. *Atween,* between. *Awthor,* author. *Ax,* ask. *Ax'd,* or *axt,* asked: thus Tyndale uses the 'word *ared* for *asked* in both editions of his translation of the New Testament. *Axin'*, asking ; particularly applied to *axing tit t' chetch*; or "asking to the church,"—that is, publishing the banns of matrimony. Thus I have known a man go to the late Mr. Cole, who for thirty-four years was the respected parish clerk of Stokesley, and say to him :—" Ah, say, Mister Kooal, Ah want *t' axins* put oop atween me an' a yung wumman." *Az*, as. *Ay*, yes.

Bahbel, Bible. *Bahbels*, Bibles. *Bahd*, bide, remain, contain oneself. *Bain*, or *bairn*, child ; oftener applied at birth to a boy, but generally used for either sex. *Bains*, or *bairns*, children of either sex. *Baptahz'd*, baptized. *Barrils*, barrels. *Be*, by; thus in Tyndale's first edition of his New Testament (1525-6) we have, "which is, as moche to saye *be* interpretacion, as God with vs," altered in the second edition (1534) to, "which is *by* interpretacion God with vs." *Beck*, brook, a natural stream of water less than a river. *Beeaks*, books. *Beeards*, beards. *Beeast*, beast. *Beeath*, both. *Beeats*, beats. *Beeld*, build. *Beeldin'*, building. *Beelt*, built. *Beer*, bear. *Beers*, bears. *Beez*, bees. *Beezom*, and *bizzom*, a broom. *Behint*, behind. *Behowld*, behold. *Bein'*, being. *Belang*, belong. *Belangs*, belongs. *Bendid*, bended. *Besahdes*, besides. *Bin*, been. *Binnd*, bind. *Blahth*, blithe, joyous, gay, cheerful. *Blaky Rig*, one of the North Yorkshire moors. *Blankits*, blankets. *Blaw*, blow. *Bleead*, blood. *Bleeam*, blame. *Blew*, blue, one of the seven primary colours. *Blews*, Blues, the wearers of blue favours in the parliamentary election, so foolishly chosen that *blue* is the conservative colour in one place, and the liberal colour in the adjoining one. *Blinkt*, blinked, gave a shy look. *Blinnd*, blind. *Blinnders*, blinders. *Bliss*, bless. *Blissid*, blessed. *Blist*, blest. *Bob*, Robert. *Bon*, burn. *Bonnin'*, burning. *Boo*, bow. *Booan*, or *booarn*, born, also borne. *Booastin'*, boasting. *Boon*, going. *Bowld*, bold. *Bowt*, bought. *Brass*, money. *Breead*, bread. *Breeak*, break. *Breeath*, breath. *Breeathe*, breathe. *Breedin'*, breeding, training. *Breet*, bright. *Breeten*, brighten. *Bricklays*, bricklayers. *Brigg*, bridge. *Brokken*, broken. *Broo*, brow. *Browt*, brought. *Brudder*, brother. *Brudders*, brothers, brethren. *Bud*, but. *Bun*, bound.

Callin', calling, shouting for, speaking ill of. *Callt*, called. *Can't*, *cahn't*, and *cannut*, can not. *Captivs*, captives, slaves. *Carin'*, heeding. *Carpin'*, carping, captious, bad to please. *Carryin'*, carrying, conveying. *Cashin*, or *cayshin*, occasion, opportunity, necessity. *Cawmly*, calmly, gently, quietly. *Cawzt*, caused, occasioned. *Censhers*, censures. *Chaige*, or *chayge*, oharge. *Changin'*, changing. *Chap*, man. *Chapil*, chapel, meeting-house. *Chass*, chase, hunt. *Chassers*, chasers, hunters. *Chassin'*, chasing, hunting. *Cheeak*, cheek, *Cheeans*, chains. *Cheer*,—"What *cheer?*" is the common mode of salutation, and means, "How are you, and how are you getting on." *Chetch*, church. *Chetch-garth*, or *chetch-yade*, church-yard. *Childer*, children, the true Dialect word being *bairns*. *Chimla*, chimney. *Chinkt*, chinked, the sound made by one coin hitting another. *Clark*, the parish clerk. *Clatter'd*, rattled, made more noise than usual. *Cleean*, clean. *Clim*, climb. *Clivver*, or *clevver*, clever, proper. *Clooas*, or *cleeas*, clothes. *Clooaser*, closer. *Cloods*, clouds. *Coashin*, caution. *Coll'd*, *Curled*. *Collidge-edicated*, educated at college. *Com*, came. *Condescendin'*, condescending, submitting to inferiors. *Confoondid*, confounded. *Confushin*, confushin. *Congregayshins*, congregations. *Conjecters*, conjectures, guesses. *Conker'd*, conquered, overcome, subdued, defeated. *Consarn*, concern. *Consarnin'*, concerning. *Consecrayshin*, consecration, rather understood in the superstitious sense of making holy by the priest than of setting apart for sacred purposes. *Contrahv'd*, contrived. *Controwl*, control. *Conversayshin*, conversation. *Convarshin*, conversion. *Cooaner*, corner. *Cooars*, course. *Cooat*, coat, also court. *Coonsil*, council, counsel. *Coonsilt*, counselled, advised. *Correctin'*, correcting, punishing, teaching aright. *Cottidge*, cottage. *Crack*, conversation, chat, gossip, boast. *Crackt*, boasted, insane. *Creeakt*, crooked. *Creedit*, credit. *Critisahz*, criticise. *Crood*, crowd. *Croodid*, crowded. *Crotshit*, crotchet, a musical term for "a note or character, equal in time to half a minim, and the double of a quaver." *Cubbert*, or *Cubbot*, the cupboard, at first a board or shelf for the cups, now applied to the closet in which crockery ware and provisions are kept. *Cud*, could. *Cuddent*, or *cud n't*, could not. *Cullers*, colours, banners, flags. *Cultivayshin*, cultivation. *Cum*, come. *Cums*, comes. *Cumm'd*, comed, become. *Cummin'*, coming. *Cumfots*, comforts. *Cumpell'd*, compelled. *Cumpleean'd*, complained. *Cumpoouser*, composure. *Cunnin'*, cunning. *Cuntrey*, or *cuntree*, country. *Curos*, or *kuros*, curious. *Curruptin'*, corrupting. *Cut*, a shorter road. *Cuttin'*, cutting.

Dad and *daddy*, childish words for father; but not more childish than the *pa* and *ma* of full grown people, who ought to be ashamed of eschewing the good old English words, "father" and "mother." *Daft*, foolish, silly, stupid, unwise. *Dag*, dug. *Dahr*, dare. *Dampt*, damped, cooled. *Dancin'*, dancing, a lively, healthy, and innocent recreation, which, although always mentioned with approval in the Bible, modern fanatics denounce as though it were a most damnable sin. *Dayleet*, daylight, clear vision. *Dazzelin'*, dazzling, overpowering by a strong light. *Deceeave*, deceive, impose on. *Dee*, die; common in the old ballads. *Deea*, do. *Deead*, dead. *Deeadly*, deadly, destructive. *Deeal*, dale: *Deean*, done. *Deea n't*, do not. *Deeath*, death. *Deed*, died. *Deer*, dear. *Deein'*, dying. *Deleet*, delight, great pleasure. *Deleetin'*, delightsome, delightful, very pleasing. *Delushin*, or *delewshin*, delusion, deception. *Delivver*, deliver, set free. *Dereckshins*, directions. *Desait*, *dissait*, and *diseeat*, deceit, deception, hypocrisy. *Dessot*, desert; a wild, barren, uncultivated, and uninhabited district. *Destruckshin*, or *distruckshin*, destruction. *Det*, debt; the true mode of pronouncing the word, and why not of spelling it? *Detarmin'd*, determined. *Devoor*, devour, worry, eat up. *Diddent*, or *did n't*, did not. *Diffend*, defend. *Ding*, knock. *Dinnot*, do not, same as *deea n't*. *Disahn'd*, designed, delineated, intended for. *Diskuvver'd*, discovered, found out. *Dispahz*, despise. *Dispair*, despair, which ETA MAWR calls "the last, the worst of errors!" *Disposhission*, disposition. *Divahn*, divine. *Diz*, does. *Dizgahz*, disguise. *Dizmal*, dismal, horrible. *Dizzent*, or *diz n't*, does not. *Doctrin*, doctrine. *Dooher*, and *dour*, door. *Doon*, down. *Doonfall*, downfall. *Doonjins*, dungeons. *Doot*, doubt. *Dowters*, daughters. *Dragon*, a common name for a cart horse, same as *Farmer*, *Jolly*, *Captain*. *Drahv*, drive. *Drayve*, drove. *Dreead*, dread, great fear. *Dreeaded*, dreaded, much feared. *Dreeadful*, full of dread, fearful. *Dreeam*, dream. *Driss*, dress. *Drisst*, dressed. *Duffil*, duffel, which NUTTALL defines as "a thick, coarse kind of wollen cloth, having a thick nap or frieze;" and which I take to be here meant for the self-coloured yarn, formerly spun from the wool of the mountain sheep in Cleveland, and wove into cloth in the district, when domestic manufacturers were more common, and luxury comparatively unknown, but when industrious people found it less difficult to make a living than their descendents do in this year of our Lord 1878. *Dyke*, ditch.

Eddicated, educated. *E'e*, eye; common in the old ballads, which are not sufficiently read: *Eeach*, each. *Eeager*, eager. *Eeagil's*, belonging to an eagle. *Feasby*, Easby. *Feast*, east. *Eeasy*, easy. *Eeat*, eat. *Een*, and *e'es*, eyes. *Een's*, eyes are. *Eeghty*, eighty. *Effecks*, or *iffecks*, effects. *Efter*, after; a real old Scandinavian word, like many others in our Dialect. *Egzamples*, examples. *El*, the same as *'ll*, will. *Eleckshins*, elections. *'Em*, them; the *hem* of Spencer, &c. *Endeeavoured*, endeavoured. *Enoo*, before long, very soon. *Er*, or. *Erectit*, erected. *Etarnal*, eternal. *Exhooatashin*, exhortation. *Expooas*, expose. *Ey*, ay, yes.

Fadder, fayder, or *fayther,* father. *Fahm,* farm. *Fahmer,* farmer, also belonging to a fahmer. *Fahmers,* farmers. *Fahn,* fine. *Fahnly,* finely. Fahnal, final. *Fahve,* five. *Failt,* failed. *Famus,* famous, celebrated. *Fand,* found; Chaucer's *fande*. *Farder,* further. *Fareweel,* farewell. *Fark,* and *fohrk,* fork. *Fashans,* fashions. *Fashind,* fashioned. *Fause,* false, deceitful, untrue. *Fearsome,* fearful, frightful. *Feeace,* face. *Feead,* fed. *Feeam,* fame. *Feeands,* fiends, personifications of evil passions. *Feeat,* foot, feet, also feat. *Feeater,* feature. *Feedin',* feeding. *Feeght,* fight. *Feeghtin',* fighting. *Feeldz,* fields. *Fella,* fellow, man; Chaucer's *fellaw ;* the *felay* and *feloy* of the old ballads. *Fellaz,* fellows, men. *Felt,* hide, conceal, keep secret; also hid, &c *Fer,* for. *Ferbidden,* forbidden. *Fergat,* forgot. *Fergeen,* or *fergi'en,* forgiven. *Fergetten,* forgotten. *Fermal,* formal, ceremonious. *Ferseeak,* forsake. *Finnd,* find *Finnds,* finds. *Flapt,* flapped. *Flay'd,* afraid, frightened. *Flee,* fly. *Fleead,* fled, also flood. *Fleeads,* floods. *Fleean,* floor. *Fleein',* flying. *Fleeas,* flies. *Fleetin',* fleeting, passing quickly. *Floor,* flour; also flower. *Floors,* flowers. *Florrish,* flourish, blossom, thrive. *Fodder,* further ; also food for cattle, and giving cattle their food. *Fooak,* and *fooaks,* folks, people. *Fooarfaythers,* forefathers. *Fooas,* foes. *Fooast,* forced. *Forgeen,* or *forgi'en,* forgiven. *Formt,* formed. *Forrists,* forests. *Fost,* first. *Fost-rate,* first-rate. *Fotton's,* fortune's. *Fotty,* forty. *Foundashin,* foundation. *Fowt,* fought. *Fowwer,* four. *Fra,* as in Chaucer, and *fiae,* as in the old ballads, are both commonly used in the Cleveland district for "from," as is also the Dialect word *frev. Freeat,* fret, mourn. *Freeatin',* fretting, mourning. *Freeten,* frighten. *Freeten'd,* frightened. *Freyin',* frying. *Frinnd,* friend. *Frinnds,* friends. *Frinndly,* friendly. *Frinndship,* friendship. *Froon,* frown. *Frozzen,* frozen. *Fund,* found. *Funt,* font. *Funlooan,* forlorn. *Furosly,* furiously. *Futur,* future.

Gahd-posts, guide-posts ; posts which ought to be erected at the forks of every road to direct travellers the way, but for the want of a broken one being repaired, between Yearsley and Easingwold, Castillo lost his way, and was glad to shelter all night in a cow-shed,—

> " And there on strawy pavement try to sleep ;
> Or, like a thief, to watch the morning light,
> And keep himself conceal'd from human sight ;
> Then snugly slip away."—See his *Local Poems*.

Gahin', or *gannin'*, going. *Gains*, distance saved in travelling by taking a shorter road than ordinary. *Gallas*, gallows : *gallasses* is also a Dialect word for the braces worn by men to keep up their trousers. *Gam*, game. *Gammelin'*, gambling. *Gams*, games. *Gan*, go : the *gang* of the old ballads, which Castillo also occasionally uses. *Gannin'*, going. *Gans*, goes. *Gardin*, garden. *Garman*, German. *Garmints*, garments, clothing. *Gat*, got. *Gav*, gave. *Gear*, or *geer*. worldly goods, furniture, raiment; used by Spenser, Shakspere, the old ballad writers, &c. *Geean*, gone; the *gune* of the old ballads. *Geean'd*, gained, won, saved, arrived at. *Geeans*, gains. *Geeapin'*, gaping. *Geen*, or *gi'en*, given. *Geeorge*, George. *Geers*, traces, or straps used in yoking horses. *Gen'ral*, general. *Gentilmen*, gentlemen; in this district, as elsewhere, generally mis-applied to any rich man. *Gess*, grass. *Gether'd*, or *gedder'd*, gathered. *Getten*, got. *Gi'es*, or *giz*, gives. *Ginnees*, guineas; English gold coins, so called from being at first coined from gold brought from the coast of Guinea, in Africa, in 1673, and which for several years rose to be of thirty shillings value, but from 1717 to 1817, when the issue of sovereigns caused them to cease to circulate, were fixed by parliament at their original value, twenty-one shillings. *Git*, get, obtain, procure, arrive. *Gits*, gets. *Giv*, give. *Givin'*, giving. *Glaisdill*, Glaisdale. *Gleeam'd*, gleamed. *Glittert*, glittered. *Glooary*, glory. *Glooaryas*, or *gloryaz*, glorious. *Glowin'*, glowing. *Goa*, or *gooa*, go. *Goadland*, Goadland, or Goathland, in Pickering-Lythe. *Goons*, gowns. *Gowld*, gold. *Graith*, condition. *Graw*, or *growh*, grow. *Grawz*, or *growhz*, grows. *Greeat*, and *grit*, great. *Greetin'*, fretting, mourning, making lamentation. *Grog* (defined in English dictionaries as "a mixture of spirit and water not sweetened,") is in Cleveland 'applied to any spirit mixed with hot water and sugar, but originally meant that of rum only. *Groops*, groups. *Grooz*, grouse, the heath-cock, or moor game. *Growhin'*, growing. *Grund*, ground. *Grunders*, grinders, the molar teeth. *Gud*, good. *Gud-like*, good-looking.

Ha', *ha'e*, and *hev*, have. *Hahm*, ham. *Hahv*, hive. *Hailsteeans*, hailstones. *Hale*, come from. *Han'*, hand. *Hans*, hands. *Happent*, happened. *Happrons*, aprons. *Hardin'*, harden. *Harness*, armour, as in Spenser, Shakspere, Dryden, &c. *Har n't*, are not. *Harpin*, harping, playing too much on one string. *Hart*, and *hairt*, heart. *Hartoft*, a hamlet between Rosedale Abbey and Pickering. *Harvist's*, harvest is. *Hawf*, half. *Hed*, had. *He 'd*, he had. *Heead*, head. *Heeal'd*, healed. *Heeam*, and *yam*, home. *Heeam-bun'*, home-bound, tied to home. *Heeaps*, heaps. *Heeard*, or *heerd*, heard, listened to. *Heeards*, herds. *Heearth*, hearth. *Heeathen*, heathen, pagan. *Heeaven*, heaven. *Heegh*, high. *Heegher*, higher. *Heegh-fleein'*, high-flying, hard-riding. *Heegh up*, high up. *Heer*, and *heher*, here. *He'll*, he will. *Helpin'*, helping, aiding, assisting. *Hennet*, *ha'e n't*, *hevvent*, and *hev n't*, have not. *Here-efter*, hereafter. *Hevvy*, heavy. *Hez*, has. *He'z*, he has, he is. *Hez n't*, has not. *Hilth*, health. *Hilthy*, healthy. *Hing*, hang. *Hings*, hangs. *Hiz*, his. *Hiz sel'*, or *hissel'*, himself. *Hod*, hold. *Hods*, holds. *Hommidge*, homage. *Honnor*, honour. *Honnorubbel*, honourable *Hoo*, how. *Hooally*, holy, sacred, religious. *Hooar*, hoar. *Hooary*, hoary. *Hoos*, house. *Hooshod*, household. *Hospitubbel*, hospitable. *Hoss*, horse. *Hosses*, horses. *Howivver*, howevver. *Howp*, hope. *Howp'd*, hoped. *Howsin'*, or *hoosin'*, household. *Hummel-jummel*, jumbled together, a motley mixture. *Hurrey*, hurry.

I', in. *Idees*, ideas. *If't*, if it. *If t'*, if the. *Impedence*, impudence. *Implooarin'*, imploaring, beseeching. *Inchantit*, enchanted. *Inclahn'd*, inclined. *Increeast*, increased, multiplied. *Indignayshin*, indignation. *Inkorridged*, encouraged. *Inglan's*, or *Inglin's*, England's. *Inrooads*, inroads. *Inscripshin*, inscription. *Insinewashins*, insinuations. *In't*, in it. *Int'*, in the. *Inte*, or *intiv*, into. *Invenshin*, invention. *Is*, often used for are. *Iskeeapt*, escaped. *Itchin'*, itching, longing for something novel. *It'll*, it will. *Itz*, its. *It'z*, it is. *It'z t'*, it is the. *Iv*, in. *Ivver*, or *ivvor*, ever. *Ivvery*, every. *Ivverlastin'*, everlasting.

Jamaica, rum, so called from the island from which it is imported. *Jesters*, gestures. *Jim*, James. *Jigs*, tricks, pranks, *Jist*, just. *Joe*, and *Jooasuff*, Joseph. *Jooavil*, jovial. *Judishus*, judicious. *Judgin'*, being judged, fair trial. *Jumpin'*, jumping, leaping. *Jurisdickshin*, jurisdiction.

Kade, card. *Kaff*, chaff. *Kahnd*, kind, affectionate, sort. *Kahnds*, kinds, sorts, varieties. *Kahndness*, kindness. *Kawd*, cold. *Keean*, keen. *Keeas*, or *keease*, case. *Ken*, know. *Kessenmas*, *Kessamas*, or *Kessmas*, Christmas; the ancient Yuletide. *Kest*, cast. *Kilt*, killed. *Kirk*, church. *Knaw*, know. *Knawn*, or *knooan*, known, ascertained. *Knaws*, knows. *Koase*, or *kaws*, cause, occasion. *Koffin'*, coughing. *Kom*, came. *Kooalpits*, coalpits. *Kooan*, corn. *Koss*, curse. *Kud*, could. *Kumpulshin*, compulsion. *Kuros*, curious. *Ky*, or *kye*, cows. *Kyqhsteean*, keystone, the middle stone of an arch.

Laber'd, laboured. *Laddie*, boy, one keen of anything. *Laff*, laugh. *Laffin'*, laughing. *Laffs*, laughs. *Lafft*, laughed. *Lafter*, laughter. *Lahk*, like. *Lahkly*, or *lahklee*, likely. *Lahn*, line. *Lahn'd*, lined. *Lahtle*, or *lahteell*, little. *Lan'*, land. *Lang*, long. *Lang'd*, longed. *Langest*, or *langist*, longest. *Langher*, longer. *Langin'*, longing. *Languish*, or *langwish*, language. *Lanlords*, landlords. *Lap*, wrap, enfold; as in Spenser, Shakspere, Milton, Dryden, &c. *Larn*, learn. *Larnin'*, learning. *Lastin'*, lasting, enduring, continuing. *Layber'd*, laboured. *Laybern'*, labouring. *Lee*, lie, falsehood, also to tell a lie. *Leeact*, laced. *Leead*, lead. *Leeads*, leads. *Leeaf*, leaf. *Leeak*, look. *Leeaks*, looks. *Leeakt*, looked. *Leealholm*, Lealholm Bridge, where Castillo resided, formerly a chapelry in the parish of Danby, now a separate parish. *Leeam*, lame. *Leeam'd*, lamed. *Leeap*, leap, jump. *Leeast*, least. *Leeat*, late. *Leeatly*, lately. *Leeav*, or *leeave*, leave. *Lejins*, legions. *Lens*, lends. *Leet*, light; Chaucer's *leite*: thus, for instance, he has *thunder-leite* for lightning. *Leets*, lights. *Lig*, lie, lay. *Ligg'd*, laid. *Ligs*, lays. *Lim*, limb. *Ling*, heather; principally applied to the *Calluna vulgaris*. *Linkt*, linked, arm-in-arm. *Lit*, let, also lighted. *Liv*, live. *Livin'*, living. *Looa*, or *law*, low. *Looashin*, lotion. *Lood*, loud. *Loss*, lose. *Lowse*, loose. *Lugs*, ears. *Lunnon*, London. *Luv*, love. *Luv'd*, loved, beloved. *Luvers*, lovers. *Lygh*, scythe.

Ma (pronounced short), me; also a common abbreviation of may. *Mah*, my. *Mahl*, mile, also used for miles. *Mahn*, mine, my own. *Mahnd*, mind. *Mair*, more, as in the old ballads. *Maister*, the old form of master, common in Chaucer, &c. *Mak*, make. *Maks*, makes. *Makkin'*, or *mackin'*, making. *Mallas*, malice. *Manhud*, manhood. *Mankahnd*, mankind. *Marcy*, or *marsy*, mercy. *Markit*, market, also to bargain. *Markit-pleeace*, market-place. *Markt*, marked. *Marraw*, marrow, pith. *Mat*, and *Matty*, Matthew. *Me*, my. *Mebby*, may be, perhaps, perchance. *Meditashin*, or *meditayshin*, meditation, deep thought, contemplation. *Meead*, made. *Meean*, mean, also applied to the moon. *Meeanin'*, meaning. *Meeason*, mason. *Meeasons*, masons. *Meeastly*, mostly. *Meeat*, meat, food, but especially applied to flesh from the butcher. *Meeght*, or *meet*, might, power. *Meeghty*, mighty, powerful. *Meetins*, meetings, especially gatherings for worship. *Mella*, mellow; not drunk, but mellowed down with intoxicating drinks,—what BURNS terms "nae that fou, but just a drappie in our e'e." *Meltit*, melted, dissolved. *Mendid*, mended, repaired. *Mesel'*, and *me-sen'*, myself. *Methody*, or *Mettardy*, Methodist, Wesleyan. *Methodys*, or *Mettodys*, Methodists, followers of John Wesley. *Misfotten's*, misfortune's. *Missin'*, missing. *Misteean*, mistaken. *Mitch*, much; Chaucer's *myche*. *Mixin'*, mixing. *Modder*, murder. *Modist*, or *moddist*, modest. *Mon*, mourn, also men. *Monnin'*, mourning. *Monny*, many. *Monney*, or *munney*, money. *Mooant*, must not. *Mooars*, moors, hills covered with ling. *Mooat*, mote, also moat. *Moont*, mount. *Moonted*. or *moontid*, mounted. *Moontin'*. mounting, ascending, climbing : also the local pronunciation of mountain. *Mottifacashin*, or *mottifacayshin*. mortification. *Mowlded*, moulded. *Mud*, might. *Mudder*, or *mudher*, mother. *Mudders*. or *mudhers*, mothers. *Mun*, must, as in the old ballads, where it also appears as *maun*. *Mutuwal*, mutual. *Muv*, move.

Narraw, or *narra*, narrow. *Narves*, nerves. *Nashin*, or *nayshin*, nation. *Natches*, notches. nicks. *Neea*, or *neeah*, no. *Neeam*, name. *Neeun*, none ; the *nane* of the old ballads : it is also used for noon. *Need n't*, need not. *Neegh*, nigh. *Neen,* nine. *Neet*, or *neeght*, night. *Neets*, nights. *Ner*, nor, also sometimes used for than. *Nighbers*, neighbours. *Nighberhud*, neighbourhood. *Nighberin'*, neighbouring. *Nimmel*, nimble. *Nivver*, never. *Nobbut*, only. *Noo*, now. *Nooatis*, or *nooatice*, notice. *Nor-eeast*, North-east, the winds from which are very keen on the Cleveland coast. *Nowble*, or *nowbel*, noble. *Nowder*, or *nowther*, neither ; Chaucer's *nouther*. *Nowt*, nothing ; the *nout* and *nocht* of the old ballads. *Numeres*, numerous, in great numbers. *Nut*, not.

O', used as a contraction both for of and on. *Offen*, and *offens*, often, oft-times. *Ommest*, almost. *On*, sometimes used for of. *Onder*, under. *Onderneeath*, underneath. *Ondersteead*, understood. *Onny*, any ; the *ony* of the old ballads. *Ooades*, order. *Ooashin*, ocean. *Oop*, up. *Oor*, our. *Oors*, ours. *Oot*, out. *Oppen*, open. *Oppen'd*, opened. *Opposishin*, or *opposisshin*, opposition. *Oppresshin*, oppression. *Ootweyh*, or *ootweygh*, outweigh. *Ordinayshin*, ordination. *Orringe*, orange. *Orringes*, or *orringiz*, oranges. *Ov*, of. *Owt*, anything. *Owther*, or *owder*, either ; Chaucer's *outher*. *Ower*, or *owwer*, over ; the *ower* and *owre* of the old ballads. *Owwerwhelm*, overwhelm. *Owwerton*, overturn. *Owwerthraw*, overthrow. *Owwerthrew*, overthrew.

Pahson, parson, clergyman. *Pahsons*, parsons. clergymen. *Pahson's*, belonging to the clergy. *Pait*, part. *Paited*, or *paitid*, parted. *Pardin*, pardon. *Parleyment*, parliament. *Parpos*, purpose. *Parsecution*, persecution. *Passidge*, passage. *Pastahm*, pastime. *Pastur*, pasture ; a field in grass where cattle are fed, not a meadow,—a distinction Dr. Watts has not borne in mind, or he never would have written " Abroad in the *meadows* to see the young lambs." *Pat*, ready, off-hand, not to seek when wanted. *Patch*, the name of a dog. *Patchwark*. patchwork. *Peeans*, pains. *Peehers*, pears. favourite fruit with the Greeks before Homer's time, and probably first introduced into Cleveland by the Romans, though the monks were afterwards our greatest horticulturalists. *Peepel*, people. *Peepel's*, belonging to the people. *Perceeav*, perceive, discern. *Pernishous*, *pernishas*, and *pahnishas*, pernicious, very injurious. *Persews*, and *parsews*, pursues. *Perswashin*, or *perswayshin*, and *parswayshin*, persuasion. *Pertend*, and *partend*, pretend. *Petishin'*, petition. *Petishins*, petitions. *Pickerin'*, Pickering. *Pickin'*, picking. *Pilgram*, pilgrim. *Pillahs*, pillars, also pillows. *Pipe*, windpipe. *Plain*, common looking, ordinary. *Plaisters*, the old English name for plasters. *Pleeace*. place. *Pleeaces*, places. *Pleeact*, placed. *Pleeads*, pleads. *Pleease*, or *pleeaz*, please. *Pleeasin'*, pleasing. *Pleaz'd*, pleased. *Plew*, plough. *Plisher*, or *plizher*, and *pleeazher*, pleasure. *Plissent*, or *plizent*, and *pleeazent*, pleasant. *Pockit*, pocket. *Polytical*, political. *Pooatch*, porch, also poach. *Pooats*, ports. *Pooblick*, public. *Pooch*, pouch. *Pooer*, *poohei*, or *poowei*, poor, also power. *Pool*, pull. *Poolpit*, pulpit. *Poot*, put. *Popt*, popped. *Posativ*, or *possativ*, positive. *Poss*, purse. *Powl*, pole, also poll. *Prahz*, or *prahze*, prize. *Prancin'*, prancing. *Preeach*, preach. *Preeachei*, preacher. *Preeachers*, preachers. *Preeaches*, preeaches. *Preeachin'*, preaching. *Preeafs*, proofs. *Pieear*, prayer. *Preeasts*, priests. *Preeasthud*, priesthood. *Preeav*, or *preev*, prove. *Prejudiz*, prejudice. *Prentis*, apprentice. *Presumpteous*, presumptious. *Preveeal*, prevail. *Prissent* present. *Pritty*, pretty. *Prizence*, presence. *Proceedins*, or *prosseedins*, proceedings. *Procleeam*, proclaim. *Prodistans*, Protestants. *Profeean'd*, profaned. *Proffits*, prophets. *Promist*, promised. *Promooat*, promote. *Promooashin*, or *promoshin*, promotion. *Prooan*, prone, inclined. *Prood*, proud. *Prophecee*, or *proficee*, prophecy. *Propper*, proper, fit, correct. *Proppertee*, property. *Props*, posts to support a tent, supports. *Pross*, chat, talk, conversation. *Prosperitee*, or *prossperitee*, prosperity. *Prosselite*, proselyte, a new convert. *Proteckshin*, protection; some years ago fearfully misapplied to the breadtax, which the farmers of the district were so deluded into the belief that it was necessary for the very existence of English agriculture, that they refused to trade with the writer of this Glossary because he had been able to penetrate the mental fog in which he had been bred, and was publicly advocating what proved to be their best interests. *Provooak*, provoke. *Pruv.* prove; rather a provincial pronunciation than anything else,— the true Dialect word being *preeav*. *Pumpos*, pompous.

Qnahter, quarter. *Queston*, question.

Rade, rode. *Rahd*, ride. *Rahders*, riders. *Rahdin'*, riding.

Rahz, or *rahze*, rise, also raise. *Raist*, or *raiz'd*, rose, raised, elevated. *Rank*, thick, numerous, near together; also stinking. *Ranter*, Primitive Methodist. *Rap*, curse, use bad language. *Raritee*, uncommon sight, something unusual. *Rayder*, rather. *Reckont*, reckoned, calculated, accounted. *Recooader*, recorder. *Reeaces*, races. *Reeach*, reach. *Reeacht*, reached. *Reeadin'*, reading. *Readins*, readings, things read. *Reeallie*, and *reeallee*, really, truly. *Reean*, rein, reign, and rain. *Reeasty*, rusty, hoarse. *Reeazt*, raised, elevated, lifted up. *Reet*, right, also cartwright. *Reeteousniss*, righteousness. *Reetly*, rightly, correctly. *Refahn'd*, refined. *Regilate*, regulate. *Relidjous*, religious. *Remahnd*, remind. *Remeean'd*, remained. *Repetashin*, or *repetayshin*, reputation. *Repooat*, report. *Repreeaf*, reproof. *Repreeav*, reprove, also reprieve. *Revarse*, reverse. *Reveeal*, reveal. *Revealt*, revealed, made known. *Revil*, or *revvil*, revel. *Rew*, rue. *Rezooat*, resort. *Rickollect*, recollect, remember. *Riddy*, ready. *Rig*, ridge. *Riggle*, or *riggel*, wriggle. *Riggin'*, the roof of the house: thus BURNS, in the opening of his fine poem, "The Vision," describes himself seated by the ingle of his "auld clay biggin'," and hearing "the restless rattons squeak about the *riggin'*." *Rigs*, or *riggs*, pranks, also ridges. *Rint*, rent; probably this word may be a comparatively modern importation. *Rispecks*, respects. *Rist*, rest. *Riverence's*, belonging to the clergyman. *Romans*, Roman Catholics. *Rooad*, road. *Rooam*, room. *Rooamantic*, romantic. *Rooar*, roar. *Rooasdill*, Rosedale. *Rooasy*, rosy. *Roond*, round. *Roozt*, roused. *Rowlin'*, rolling. *Rowl'd*, rolled. *Ruff*, rough. *Ruint*, ruined. *Rulin'*, ruling. *Rummellin'*, rumbling. *Runnin'*, running. *Runsick*, Runswick, a beautiful bay on the Cleveland coast.

Sahd, side. *Sahkel*, circle. *Sahlance*, silence. *Sahlent*, silent. *Sahn*, since; Chaucer's *syn*. *Sahn'd*, signed. *Sahserdooatal*, sacerdotal, priestly. *Sair*, sore. *Sal*, or *sall*, shall, as in Chaucer and the old ballads. *Salvashin*, or *salvayshin*, salvation. *Sampel*, sample. *Sampels*, samples. *Sang*, song, sung. *Sangshin*, or *sankshin*, sanction. *Sangshinn'd*, or *sankshinn'd*, sanctioned. *Sarch*, search. *Sarcht*, searched. *Sarmon*, or *sahmon*, sermon. *Sarpant*, *sahpent*, and *sarpint*, serpent; his Satanic Majesty. *Sarten*, or *sartin*, certain. *Sarvant*, or *sahvant*, servant. *Sarvants*, or *sahvants*, servants. *Sarves*, or *sahves*, serves. *Sarvice*, or *sahvis*, service. *Sarvt*, served. *Sattan*, or *Satton*, the old English name of Satan; the personification of evil. *Sattan's*, belonging to the devil. *Savin'*, the true Dialect being *seeavin'*, saving. *Saw*, sow, to scatter seed for growth. *Sawn*, sown. *Saxon*, sexton. *Saxon's*, belonging

to the sexton. *Scampert*, scampered. *Scar*, scare, frighten.
Sceeals, or *skeeals*, scales. *Scholard*, or *schollard*, scholar.
Scooan'd, scorned. *Scrahb*, scribe. *Scripter*, scripture, Bible.
Sed, said. *Seea*, or *seeah*, so; the *sa* and *sae* of the old ballads.
Seeacrit, secrit. *Seeaf*, safe. *Seeak*, seek, also sake. *Seeal*,
seal, also sale. *Seeam*, seem, appear, also seam. *Seeams*,
seems, appears, also seams. *Seean*, soon. *Seeav*, or *seeave*,
save, also sieve, and the rush (*junters*). *Seeaven*, seven.
Seeaz'd, and *seeazt*, seized. *Seed*, saw. *Seein'*, seeing. *Sel'*,
self, as in the old ballads. *Seer*, and *sewer*, sure. *Seerly*, *seer-
lie*, and *sewerlie*, surely. *Seerous*, or *seeros*, serious. *Seet*, sight.
Seez, sees. *Self-devooashin*, self-devotion. *Sen*, since, as in
Chaucer and the old ballads. *Serprahz*, and *supprahz*, surprise.
Settisfackshin, satisfaction. *Settisfied*, satisfied. *Settin'*, set-
ting. *Sewin'*, sewing, pronounced as spelled, as all words *ought*
to be. *Shahn*, shine. *Sham*, shame. *Shamm'd*, shamed, as-
hamed, also acted the hypocrite. *Shanks*, legs. *Shap*, shape.
Sheea, she. *Shivverin'*, shivering, trembling. *Shockt*, shocked.
Shooan, shone. *Shooat*, short. *Shooders*, shoulders. *Sike*,
such. *Silversahd*, silverside. *Silvert*, silvered. *Simmibreeaves*,
semibreves, notes in music, equal to two minims, to four crot-
chets, and to eight quavers. *Singin'*, singing. *Sirkalashin*, or
Sirkalayshin, circulation. *Sirkit*, circuit. *Skaihs*, skies.
Skooars, scores. *Sleeght*, slight. *Slipt*, slipped. *Smahl'd*,
smiled. *Smahlin'*, smiling. *Smeeaky*, smoky. *Smiddy*, smithy.
Snaw, snow. *Snooarin'*, snoring. *Sockit*, socket. *Soilt*, soiled.
Sollem, solemn. *Sooas*, source. *Sooat*, sort. *Soobjeck*, sub-
ject. *Soobjeck 's*, subject is. *Soobjecks*, subjects. *Soobscripshin*,
subscriptson. *Soobstance*, substance. *Soobtel*, subtle. *Soond*,
sound. *Soonded*, and *soondid*, sounded. *Sorvay*, survey.
Soshalism, socialism, which Castillo, like many more, errone-
ously associates with heterodoxy in religion. *Sov'rans*, sove-
reigns, pounds sterling. *Sowl*, soul. *Sowls*, souls. *Spak*,
spoke, the old *spake*. *Speeach*, speech. *Speeak*, speak. *Sperits*,
or *sperrits*, spirits. *Sperrit 's*, belonging to the soul. *Spice*,
gingerbread. *Spinnd*, spend. *Spooat*, sport, fun, merriment.
Spooats, sports. *Spoor*, spur. *Spoort*, spurred. *Spoilt*, spoiled.
Spreed, and *spreead*, spread. *Staff*, a walking stick, standing
up, like *Awd Ahzaak's*, "aboon hiz hand, t' awd fashin'd way."
Stan', stand. *Standart*, standard. *Stang*, stung. *Starvin'*,
starving, perishing for want of the necessaries of life. *Steead*,
stood. *Steeaks*, stakes. *Steeal*, steal, also stool. *Steean*, stone;
the *stean* of Spenser, the *stone* and *stean* of the old ballads, &c.
Steeans, stones. *Steepel-chass*, steeple-chase, defined by NUT-
TALL as "a race between a number of horsemen, to see which

can first reach some distant object in a straight course," and
however objectionable, having no connection with the church,
as Castillo seems to have imagined. *Steepel-hoos*, "steeple-
house," the name applied to churches by George Fox, but not
a Cleveland expression. *Steers*, Staithes, a large and most
romantic fishing village on the Cleveland coast. *Stewhads*,
stewards. *Stiddy*, steady. *Stock*, father of a family. *Stooary*,
story. *Stooary'z*, story is. *Stootest*, or *stootist*, stoutest,
strongest. *Stop*, stay. *Stoppin'*, staying, residing. *Stour*, dust
blowing about. *Stowsla'*, Stokesley. *Straave*, or *strayve*, strove.
Strahr, strive. *Strang*, strong. *Strangher*, stronger. *Strather*,
fuss, commotion. *Stright*, straight, right, not crooked. *Stript*,
stripped, undressed. *Submisshin*, or *submishin*, submission.
Succeshin, or *suckshesshin*, succession. *Sud*, should, ought to
do. *Sum*, some; as in the old ballads, &c. *Sumboddy*, some-
body, some person. *Sumtahms*, sometimes, occasionally.
Sunda's, Sunday's, belonging to the Christian Sabbath. *Suns*,
sons. *Suppoat*, support. *Supprahzes*, surprises. *Surroond*,
surround. *Swap*, exchange, barter. *Sweear*, or *sweer*, swear.
Sweearin', or *sweerin'*, swearing. *Sweeat*, sweat, perspire, per-
spiration. *Sweeaty*, sweaty, perspiring, wet with perspiration.
Sweethart, sweetheart, lover, an old English term of endear-
ment. *Swiggin'*, drinking copiously. *Swooan*, sworn.

'T, it. *T'*, or *th'*, the; a very common contraction of the
definite article, which is never fully pronounced by those who
speak the dialect; thus, the apple is, *t' happel*; the children, *t'
bairns'*; the church, *t' chetch*, &c. (In Chaucer we have, *tham-
bassiatours*, for the ambassadors; *thexecucion*, for the execu-
tion; *thwitel*, for the whittle or knife, &c.) *Tackin'*, or *takkin'*,
taking, agitated state of mind. *Tahm*, time. *Tak*, take; also
used for ill flavour. *Taks*, takes.. *Tasshils*, tassels. *Te*, to.
Teea, or *teeah*, too. *Teeabels*, tables. *Teeach*, teach. *Teeak*,
took; the *tuik* and *tuke* of the old ballads. *Teeal*, tale. *Teean*,
taken, tune, the one; the context will always show in which of
these various meanings it is used. *Teld*, and *telt*, told. *Tha*,
they, thee, thou. *Tha 're*, they are. *Tha 've*, they have.
Thare, *theer*, and *ther*, are often used indiscriminately for there
and for their. *The*, and *de*, thy. *Theeam*, theme. *Theerfooar*,
and *therefooar*, therefore. *Theease*, and *deease*, these, those.
Thenk, thank. *Ther*, their, as in the old ballads; also there,
and they are. *Thoff*, though. *Thoo*, and *doo*, thou. *Thooas*,
thooaz, and *dooaz*, those. *Thoosans*, thousands. *Thosty*, thirsty.
Thowt, thought. *Thowts*, thoughts. *Thowtful*, thoughtful.
Thravin', thriving. *Thrawin'*, throwing. *Threead-bare*, thread-
bare. *Threeatens*, threatens. *Threeats*, threats. *Throo*, and

thruff, through. *Thunner*, |thunder. *Thunner'd*, thundered.
Till, and *tell*, until. *Ti 't*, to it, to the. *Tire*, the metal orna-
ments of a coffin, which, according to a foolish old Cleveland
superstition, when procured from a grave and made into finger-
rings, are a certain cure for the cramp to all who wear them:
for some amusing anecdotes anent which delusion see the
People's History of Cleveland, and also the *North of England
Illustrated Annual*. *Tiv*, to. *Toke*, or *tawk*, talk, converse,
conversation. *Tom*, and *Tommy*, Thomas. *Ton*, or *tonn*, turn.
Tonn'd, turned. *Tonnin'*, turning; also the turn or bend in a
road or highway. *Tooach*, torch. *Towt*, taught. *Travil*,
travel. *Treead*, tread, also trade. *Trew*, true. *Trew drawin'*,
pulling equally. *Trewly*, truly. *Trewth*, truth. *Trist*, trust.
Tristy, trusty. *Trizher*, treasure. *Trumpits*, trumpets. *Tryin'*,
trying. *Tummel*, tumble. *Twahnd*, twined, entwined. *Tweea*,
two; the *tway* of Spenser, and the *twa* of the old ballads.
Twist, turn.

Udders, or *udhers*, others; the *uthers* of the old ballads. *Unah-
deean'd*, not ordained. *Unkahnd*, unkind. *Upbreead*, upbraid.
Uz, us.

Vanitee, vanity. *Varra*, and *varry*, very. *Vast*, great deal,
large quantity, great number. *Vext*, vexed. *Vinnerubbel*,
venerable. *Vooat*, vote.

Wa, or *wah* (pronounced short), we. *Wacken*, or *wakken*,
waken, awake. *Wacken'd*, or *wakken'd*, wakened, awakened.
Wad, would, as in the old ballads, &c. *Wad n't*, would not.
Wahd, wide. *Wahn'd*, warned. *Wahnin'*, or *warnin'*, warning.
Wahse, or *wahz*, wise. *Wahser*, or *wahzer*, wiser. *Wanner'd*,
wandered. *Wark*, work, also ache. *Warld*, world. *Warldly*,
worldly. *Warld's*, world's, belonging to the world. *Warshop*,
worship. *Warthies*, worthies. *Warrihers*, warriors. *Waz*,
was; often used for were. *Wedder*, whether, also weather.
Weddercock, weathercock. *Weea*, *weeah*, *wheea*, or *wheeah*, who;
the *wha* of the old ballads. *Weeak*, week, also, weak. *Weean't*,
will not. *Weeary*, weary. *Weeast*, waste, also waist. *Weel*,
well, as in the old ballads, &c. *Wer*, were, our. *Wershoppers*,
or *wosshoppers*, worshippers. *Whahl*, wile, whilst, until; the
whiles of Shakspere. *Whativver*, whatever. *Wheeas*, or
wheeaz, whose. ' *Wherivver*, wherever. *Whilk*, which. *Whohl*,
whirl. *Whoor*, where. *Whyah*, very well, I am willing. *Wi'*,
with, as in the old ballads. *Wickid*, wicked, sinful. *Wilthy*,
wealthy. *Wimmin*, women. *Winda*, and *winder*, window.
Winnd, wind. *Winnot*, will not. *Wiv*, with. *Wivoot*, without.
Woak, or *woke*, walk. *Woaks*, or *wokes*, walks. *Wod*, word.
Wolld, world. *Wonner*, and *wunner*, wonder. *Wonner'd*, won-

nert, wunner'd, and *wunnert,* wondered. *Worhk,* work. *Wrang,* wrong.

Ya (sounded short), ye, you. *Yabbel,* able. *Yack,* or *yak,* oak. *Yah,* one. *Yal,* or *yall,* ale. *Yan,* one. *Yance,* once. *Yan's,* belonging to one. *Yatton,* Ayton. *Yer,* your. *Yeth,* earth. *Yeth's,* earth's, belonging to this planet. *Yis,* yes. *Yit,* yet; used by Edmund Spenser, not merely "for the rhyme," as his commentators have ignorantly guessed, who have never taken the trouble to ascertain if there was really such a word in existence. *Yoo,* you. *Yoo've,* you have. *Youst,* and *youzt,* used, used to. *Yung,* young.

Tailpiece by Heaviside.

Such is Castillo's illustration of the North York Dialect. Should the sale be sufficient to encourage the continued publication of other works in the Dialect, the Editor hopes to follow it up with reprints of works now become scarce, as well as with original matter. Being too intimately connected with the Authoress of

Rhymes and Sketches to Illustrate the Cleveland Dialect

for his testimony to the fidelity of the work to be regarded as altogether impartial, he may be pardoned for quoting the following, culled from among many other

OPINIONS OF THE PRESS.

" A most interesting little work."—*Masonic Magazine.*

" Capital songs and stories."—*Iron.*

" Quite apart from the peculiarity of language they display, her verses are worth reading. Some of them have pathos, others have humour. Nor are they difficult to understand............Mrs. Tweddell has done for the Cleveland Dialect what the Rev. William Barnes has done for that of Dorset; she has clad its peculiarities in very pleasant verse."—*Pictorial World.*

" A clever little volume."—*Lloyd's Weekly London Newspaper.*

" A little work of considerable merit, the pieces it contains all having a tendency for good."—*City Press.*

" Mrs. Tweddell has done her work well, and the result is a bright little book, without a dry line from the beginning to the end."—*Westminster Chronicle.*

" We have read, with singular pleasure, a little book, published by Tweddell and Sons, of Stokesley, Yorkshire, and composed by the wife of our well-known Bro. G. M. Tweddell, entitled *Rhymes and Sketches to Illustrate the Cleveland Dialect.* Being, from long residence, always ready to say, ' I'se Yorkshire,' we have perused the tiny volume with the deepest interest and pleasure. Both the rhymes and the prose are equally effective and true, as we can assert from a long residence in Yorkshire. We feel sure that were several of the extracts of Mrs. Tweddell's zealous labour of love read out to a Yorkshire audience, (and this is the best of all tests as to truthfulness and effect,) great would be the applause, heartily expressed would be the admiration. One friend of ours, of many years, we hear even now, whose rendering of either the humorous or pathetic pieces, whether of 'Polly Rivers visit te Stowslay Cattle Show,' or 'The Poor Mother's Lament for her Little Bairn,' would have drawn alike smiles and tears from a warm-hearted Yorkshire gathering. Even his own inimitable story of the amiable 'Beer' and the couragous Yorkshire 'Young Wumman,' would pall in comparison before Polly's vivid description of the 'two loving doves' and their 'coo, coo, cooing.' We hope that a large circulation may encourage Mrs. Tweddell to persevere in similar efforts, as we feel sure that, like the iron-stone of pleasant Cleveland, she has struck happily on a vein of sterling 'metal,' not yet, by a great deal, exhausted, and capable of being further worked out with pleasure and with profit. We commend the *Rhymes and Sketches to illustrate the Cleveland Dialect* to the notice of all our Yorkshire readers, nay, and for the matter of that, of our 'Southerners' too."—*The (London) Freemason.*

"It is a genuine little production, marked by truth and ability, by reality and humour, by sound teaching and a good moral; and we are very glad in these days of dubious literary productions, and hesitating utterances of a higher excellence, to claim for it the approval and encouragement of all who wish the literature of the hour to fulfil its true end, the intellectual amusement and the moral edification of all classes."—*The Freemason (second notice).*

"We have quoted the above beautiful lyric ['Twea Match Lads'] from a newly published and neatly bound little volume, written by Mrs. G. M. Tweddell, of Stokesley, under the title of *Rhymes and Sketches to Illustrate the Cleveland Dialect.* Prose and verse are mixed with a master hand; each one is good, either for its humour, its pathos, or the light it throws upon such bits of country life as only well written dialect sketches can illustrate; and we have only selected the above on account of its shortness. A Glossary, written by her husband (the Yorkshire Massey), illustrates the meaning of the dialect words, some of which are puzzling even to a West Riding reader. We have no doubt that the sale will be such as will satisfy the publisher and the author that both of them have made their mark upon the literature of their county, and that both have earned the respect of that many they have for more than a quarter of a century written to and about."—*Wakefield Free Press.*

"In the little volume before us, we have a pleasant collection of homely sayings, poetic thoughts, and wholesome sketches, strung together by no mean hand and brain, in the Dialect of Cleveland, as that part of the old county of York which abuts on Durham is called...........Its sons have described its attractions,

—and it has remained for one of the daughters of this fair land, under the nom de plume of FLORENCE CLEVELAND, to embalm the prattle of its children, and the strong, homely sense of their fathers, in the vernacular Dialect of the fireside hearths. Mrs. Tweddell appropriately opens her volume with a description of ' T' Awd Cleveland Custums '............In ' Jim's Wife' and ' Sly Sally' we have other glimpses of the ideas of what the home life of these workers must be ; and, if they are not temperate people, the admonition to ' Keep Sowber,' to ' Keep Stright,' and ' Cum, Stop at Yam te Neet, Bob,' would make them so, more than a score of teetotal lectures. The prose sketches are as healthy and as pleasant as the poetic pieces. Few who care for homely English thoughts put into homely verse, will be without this little work ; whilst those who know the wolds of Yorkshire and the dales of Durham will welcome it as breathing the home tones in the home time, and will treasure it as a breath from Rosebury Topping over the country round." — *Royal Leamington Spa Courier.*

" As preserving the forms, and giving an idea of the pronunciation of many words which are becoming—some of which have already become—obsolete, and as showing the influence on the local Dialect of the Scandinavian element which once prevailed in the North-Eastern provinces, Mrs. Tweddell's compositions will be of some value in an archæological sense, while the various *Rhymes and Sketches*, looking at them as a whole, are readable and in excellent tone."—*Yorkshire Post.*

" We have been much pleased with these *Rhymes.* There is something more than jingle in them,—for they are as remarkable for their dry wit and homely philosophy as they are for their dialect and constructive skill. The fair authoress has succeeded in a task that must have been to her a labour of love. Her poetical sketches are as skilful as bits of biography, as her more serious poems are noticeable for their healthy morality. The prose pieces are quite as good as the poetry. The Sunday School Lad and the Angels is worth quoting."—*York Herald.*

" Mrs. Tweddell is the Poet Laureat of Cleveland, and her husband is an untiring local historian of no small antiquarian research, who takes a keen interest in everything that takes place in the ' Land of hills, and woods, and streams,' so eloquently apostrophised by his enthusiastic wife. The Tweddell printing press is seldom still, and although Mr. Tweddell sometimes projects more than he can accomplish, ...this is a venial error of judgement, which bears testimony to the earnestness with which he endeavours to make Stokesley the Athens of Cleveland. In the neat little volume before us, Mrs. Tweddell has sought to rescue from oblivion some of the salient features of the Cleveland Dialect.. ....Few places in the North have been subjected to such inroads from other districts. The development of the iron mines has transformed the character of her population, and attracted to the North Riding men from almost every shire in England. Hence the Cleveland Dialect is fast becoming obsolete. To rescue it from oblivion is the object of this little book, and we need hardly say that the production has been a labour of love to the talented lady who seems to make Cleveland-worship a kind of religion............From the extracts which we have given of the *Rhymes*, the reader will be able to judge of the faithfulness with which the author has rendered the Cleveland Dialect. Even those who cannot appreciate the fidelity of the rendering will yet find much to amuse and to interest in the *Rhymes* and the *Sketches* of this little volume. Mrs. Tweddell writes with freedom and ease, many of her *Rhymes* are charming little poems, and in all there is a natural grace and truthfulness which make them well worth reading for their own sake. The *Sketches* are mostly humorous, and, although not so attractive to the general reader as the *Rhymes*, may likely enough be even more popular in Cleveland. It only needs to be added that a Glossary, abridged from Mr. Tweddell's *People's History of Cleveland*, completes the value of this unassuming little work."— *Northern Echo.*

" Mrs. Tweddell has rendered good service in preparing and bringing out those *Rhymes and Sketches*, which so well illustrate not only the Dialect but the population of Cleveland before its invasion by the ironstone miners."— *Yorkshire Gazette.*

" We know not whether more to commend the intention or the execution of this little work. The iron horse is running down our local dialects. Fusing and interfusing, it makes war on the confusion of tongues, and threatens to melt them all into one; and it is a good work to give the speech of a district to the keeping of print, ere it has passed away from the local tongue. 'The only merit that is claimed' by Mrs. Tweddell for her *Rhymes and Sketches* 'is the stringing together of a good many Cleveland words and expressions that are fast becoming obsolete.' But this is a great merit, and her pages have also more. They are not only good for their purpose, but good in themselves. Prose and verse are alike good, and especially commend themselves to the approval of all who were 'to the dialect born,' some of whom knew 'awd Stowslay Toon' before the snort of the locomotive engine was heard in Cleveland, and when the iron ore still slumbered in the deep recesses of the Yorkshire hills."— *Newcastle Daily Chronicle.*

TESTIMONIAL
TO
GEORGE MARKHAM TWEDDELL.

It has long been the wish of many of the friends and admirers of this well known Author and Public Speaker, to present him with some substantial Testimonial of esteem, for his life-long Labours for the Mental and Moral Elevation of the People There has scarcely been a movement in the path of Progress which he has not aided, publicly and privately, by his tongue and pen, from his youth up to the present time; often at a great pecuniary loss to himself; so that many, who may have differed widely from him in opinion, have not hesitated to express their admiration of the enthusiastic and unflinching manner in which he has always devoted his abilities in striving to promote whatever appeared to him to be for the good of humanity, whether popular or otherwise. The present Testimonial will consist of a PURSE OF GOLD, to help him through heavy losses and family affliction, over which he has no control, and to aid him to complete those Literary Labours in which he is known to have been so long engaged; whilst to preserve an enduring record of its presentation, the names of all the Subscribers, whether of pounds or of pence, will be printed in book form, and copies deposited in all the principal public libraries, as well as distributed among the Subscribers. The Testimonial will not be of a Sectarian, Party, or even Local character; and Subscriptions for the same will be gladly received, and duly acknowledged, by

Wm. Andrews, F.R.H.S., No. 10, Colonial Street, Hull.
Charles Bell, Draper, 1, Sussex-street, Middlesbrough, and High-street, Redcar.
Isaac Binns, F.R.H.S., Borough Accountant, Batley.
R. Broadbridge, Minister of the Unsectarian Church, Wilnecote, near Tamworth.
A. J. Broadbridge, Overseer's Office, Middlesbrough.
J. Tom Burgess, F.S.A., Grassbrooke, Leamington.

W. H. Burnett, Editor of the *Daily Exchange*, Middlesbrough.
F. B. Cooke, Manager of the National Provincial Bank of England, Stokesley.
T. W. Craster, M.D., Linthorpe Road, Middlesbrough.
L. F. Crummey, M.R.C.S., Manor House, Great Ayton.
John Dixon, Merchant, Skelton, via Marske-by-the-Sea.
John Dunning, Ex-Mayor, Southfield Villas, Middlesbrough.
J. F. Elgee, Manager of Backhouse and Co's Bank, Middlesbro'.
Thomas B. Forster (Sec. to the " Wharton " Lodge, I.O. Oddfellows), 32, High-street, Skelton, Cleveland.
Joseph Gould, Printer, 24, South-street, Middlesbrough.
Spencer T. Hall, " The Sherwood Forester," Burnley.
Emra Holmes, Collector of Customs, Fowey, Cornwall.
George Kenning, Masonic Jeweller and Publisher, 198, Fleet-street, 1, 2, and 3, Little Britain, and 175, Aldersgate-street, London; 2, Monument Place, Liverpool; and 9, West Howard-street, Glasgow.
Samuel F. Longstaffe, F.R.H.S., Norton Green, Stockton-on-Tees.
John Macfarlane and Sons, Booksellers, Middlesbrough.
Wm. Mason, Berlin House, Newport Road, Middlesbrough.
David Normington, Watchmaker, Stokesley.
Rev. John Oxlee, Rector of Cowesby, via Thirsk.
Thomas Rawling (Sec. to Stokesley District I.O. Oddfellows), Stamp Office, Gisbrough.
Henry Roberts, 37, Rushford-street, Middlesbrough.
John Ryley Robinson, LL.D., Westgate, Dewsbury.
John Sutherst, Cleveland Ironworks, Gisbrough.
Fred. Wake (Sec. to Friendly Dividend Society), Carlton-in-Cleveland.
George Watson, J.P., Cleveland Villas, Middlesbrough.
Richard Watson, Manager of the Darlington District Joint Stock Bank, Stokesley.
Thomas Watson, Auctioneer, 4, Grange Road, Darlington.

———

Persons wishing to be added to the above List, are requested to send their names and addresses to

WILLIAM ANDREWS, F.R.H.S.,
Honorary Secretary.

No. 10, *Colonial Street, Hull,*
November, 1877.

2

*In one beautifully printed volume of 286 pages, crown 8vo., cloth,
gilt lettered, reduced from 5s. to 3s. 6d., or
free by bookpost 4s.*

The Story of Count Ulaski; Aurelia, or the Gifted, and other original Poems, with Translations.

By ETA MAWR.

Authoress of "Far and Near," "A Tour of Times Gone By," &c.

———

COMMENDATIONS OF ETA MAWR'S POEMS

"An eloquent volume. . . . I find much to admire in 'Count Ulaski'
and 'Aurelia,' especially the latter, and the Translations appear to me
composed with rare ease and felicity. They introduce me to many poems
with which I was before unacquainted."— Lord Lytton

"A very pleasing and delightful volume . . . The charm of metre
goes a good way with me, and I like to pause and linger over flowing and
graceful verse, and that yours most assuredly is. . . . But to return to
those two tales, 'Ulaski' and 'Aurelia,' they are full of interest, the one
of active, the other of sedentary interest, or, as the Germans would distin-
guish them, of objective and subjective interest. . . . I have read the
minor poems also with a great deal of enjoyment. The 'Sonnet to Handel'
struck me as particularly good. 'The Stocking Knitter' is a gem."— Sir
J. Herschel.

"I like your 'Aurelia' exceedingly, and your 'Golden Mean.' Your
verses are loaded with thought "—Rev. George Gilfillan.

"In the volume before us there are a thousand beauties. . . . We
really think that no fruits of the modern muse contain finer passages, or
show deeper knowledge of the human heart than 'Ulaski' and 'Aurelia.'
. . . The minor poems, both original and from the German, have genu-
ine force and sweetness. . . . The 'Poet of Coila' has never been
greeted with a more just, a more eloquent, or a more charming eulogium.
. . . The noblest efforts of Burns's genius, and the finest qualities in
those efforts, are referred to with equal warmth of admiration, and sound-
ness of critical judgment. The tributes entitled 'Gibsoniana' are warm,
genial, graceful, eloquent, and well deserved, for undoubtedly Gibson
stands on the highest roll of British sculptors."—Durham Advertiser.

"Her translations of German poetry are excellent and well selected, and,
taking her book altogether, it is decidedly an honour to the head and
heart of the authoress."—Illustrated Times.

"Here we have in a small compass a great deal of very good poetry.
. . . The present volume fully sustains, and, we think, adds in no small
degree to the reputation achieved by its predecessor."—W. T. Kime, Esq,
Barrister-at-Law, J.P., Editor of "Albert the Good," &c.

"In reviving the memory of poor Poland you have struck most forcibly
the chords of my heart, for from a very early age I have felt for its suffer-
ings a sincere sympathy."—M. G. Solling, a German correspondent.

NORTH OF ENGLAND TRACTATES.

Under the above title, the Publishers purpose to print, from time to time, a collection of small Treatises, in prose and verse, relating to the North of England, offering them to the general public at the lowest possible prices which will clear the necessary expenses of publication. The following are now ready, at One Penny Each.

No. 1.—*Cleveland*, a Poem, in Blank Verse, by JOHN REED APPLETON, F.S.A.

No. 2.—*Prince Oswy*, a Legend of Rosebury Topping, by the late JOHN WALKER ORD, F.G.S.L.

No. 3.—*The Trials and Troubles of a Tourist*, by JOHN REED APPLETON, F.R.S.N.A.; with Tailpieces by Bewick and Linton.

No. 4.—*Rhymes to Illustrate the North York Dialect*, by FLORENCE CLEVELAND.

No. 5.—*Yorkshire Worthies*, by JOHN RYLEY ROBINSON, LL.D., with Medallion of Capt. Cook.

No. 6.—*The Old, Old Woman of Elton*, a Ballad, by ETA MAWR; with Tailpiece by Linton.

No. 7.—*Cleveland Sonnets*, by GEORGE MARKHAM TWEDDELL.

No. 8.—*Halifax Gibbet and Gibbet Law*, by JOHN RYLEY ROBINSON, LL.D.; with illustrations.

No. 9.—*Howley Hall*, a Prose Sketch; and *Rosebury Topping*, a Blank Verse Poem, by JOHN RYLEY ROBINSON, LL.D.; with Tailpiece by Bewick.

No. 10.—*Sunnyside Gill*, a Blank Verse Poem, by GEORGE MARKHAM TWEDDELL, F.R.S.N.A., Copenhagen, &c.

No. 11.—*Cleveland Thoughts, or the Poetry of Toil*, a Blank Verse Poem, by ANGUS MACPHERSON, C.E.; with Tailpiece by Bewick.

No. 12.—*The Saxon Cross, Church, &c., at Dewsbury*, by JOHN RYLEY ROBINSON, LL.D.; with four fine Illustrations, and a Linton Tailpiece.

No. 13.—*Awd Gab, o' Steers; How he Tried te Sweetheart Betty Moss:* a Trew Teale, related in the North York Dialect, by FLORENCE CLEVELAND; with a Glossary.

No. 14.—*The Cleveland Knight, or Origin of English Alum Making*, a Ballad, by the late MAURICE H. DALE; with a Portrait of Lambert Russell, and a Tailpiece by Bewick.

No. 15.—*In Memoriam. On the Death of Mark Philips, Esq.*, a Blank Verse Poem, by GEORGE MARKHAM TWEDDELL.

No. 16.—*The Baron of Greystoke*, a Legendary Ballad; by the REV. JAMES HOLME, B.A., late Vicar of Kirkleatham.

No 17.—*A Voice from Flood and Fell*, by the late J. G. GRANT.

No. 18.—*Towton Field, or the "Battle of England's Civill Warres;"* by JOHN R. ROBINSON, LL.D.

Complete in one volume of 100 pages, fscp. 8vo., printed on good paper, bound in blue cloth, gilt lettered, price 1s. 6d , or strongly bound and richly ornamented, 2s. 6d.; by bookpost 2d. extra.

RHYMES AND SKETCHES TO ILLUSTRATE THE CLEVELAND DIALECT,

By Mrs. G. M. Tweddell (Florence Cleveland).

COMMENDATIONS.

From His Grace the Archbishop of York.—" An interesting volume of *Sketches.* It has, besides its poetical interest, a certain philological interest too. I am very glad to possess it "

From Robert Henry Allan Esq., F.S.A., J.P., D.L., &c., of Blackwell Hall.—" My dear Mr. Tweddell, I have received three copies of Mrs. Tweddell's elegant and clever volume. The *Sketches* are very characteristic and most amusing; and the Glossary is as essentially necessary as it is valuable. . . Will you kindly send me twenty-seven extra bound copies (2/6 each), which, with the three copies just received, will make up the thirty copies subscribed for by Mrs. Allan and myself, for which I beg leave to enclose a cheque on Messrs. Backhouse and Co. for £5, and which you will be so obliging as to hand to Mrs. Tweddell with our united compliments."

From the Rev. T. P. Williamson (formerly of Gisbrough) Vicar of Little Brickhill, Bucks., Author of *If Either—Which,* &c.—" Alluding to your Preface, I may say, that it is a happy thing that no other person *was* writing in the Cleveland Dialect at this time; for I am certain no other person could have produced so delightful a little book as yours. It is not only the 'Cleveland Dialect' very happily rendered, but the whole (whether poetry or prose) hits off the Cleveland *character* of a former day in a way that leaves nothing to be desired."

From the Rev. James Holme, B.A., late Vicar of Kirkleatham, Author of *Leisure Musings and Devotional Meditations, Mount Grace Abbey, and other Poems.*—" I have long intended to write and thank you for the beautiful little volume of your excellent rustic poems."

From Mr. J. H. Eccles, of Leeds, Author of *Yorkshire Songs,* &c.—" I like both Poems and Sketches very much, and think they are a credit both to your *head* and *heart*. . . . Believe me to be your sincere wisher, that the work may have the popularity it deserves, and dear old Cleveland furnish you with themes for many poems and sketches of such naturalness and beauty."

From William Danby, Esq , of Elmfield House, Exeter (formerly of Gisbrough), Author of *Poems,* &c.—" I received Mrs. Tweddell's book on Saturday night, and enclose stamps. It was, as Uriah Heap says, 'like the ringing of old bellses' to hear, as it were, through the void of time, the sound of the robust vernacular of my native district. . . I have already had great pleasure in reading several of the pieces, and am looking forward to the opportunity of making myself acquainted with the rest. . I can only hope that many 'Bobs' may be induced to 'stop at yam' at nights, and read Mrs. Tweddell's sound moral lessons, and occasional pathetic utterances, to their families. The railways, and the vast introduction of an abnormal population, consequent on the development of the iron trade, must have gone far to banish much of the old Dialect, and induce many natives to attempt a more cosmopolitan mode of speech; and therefore we should be the more obliged to Mrs. Tweddell for her endeavour that it should not be wholly forgotten. She has done for the North Riding what Hughes has done for Wiltshire, Barnes for Dorsetshire, 'Nathan Hogg' for Devonshire, Tregellas for Cornwall, and other writers for other counties."

From Eta Mawr, Authoress of *Far and Near, The Story of Count Ulaski, Aurelia, and other Poems*, &c.—"Accept my best thanks, my dear 'Florence Cleveland,' for the elegantly bound copy of your *Rhymes and Sketches to illustrate the Cleveland Dialect*, whose contents I had already devoured in their humbler garb, with much admiration of the skill and talent, the wit and humour, of the clever authoress, and the excellent moral tone everywhere, but unobtrusively, pervading it. . . I hope your little book will have customers among the class who speak its language, and that both wives and husbands will benefit by such moral lessons as are conveyed in 'Come, stop at yam te neet, Bob,' &c. Of the prose *Sketches* my favourite is the inimitable 'Betty Moth,' but they are all very good in their way."

From Mr. W. M. Egglestone, Author of *Weardale Forest*.— "When I came home last night, Mrs. Tweddell's Cleveland Sketches was on my table. I glanced through the work, and read 'Stowslay Cattle Show,' which pleased me very much. With some trifling exceptions, the Cleveland Dialect is very much like that of Weardale. How Bill and Polly *liked* each other, and how they bungled about expressing their love, their sweet-hearting at the gate, &c., is very much like the style how a Weardale lad and lass, twenty years ago, would have done. The sketch of 'Polly Rivers's Trip te Stowslay Cattle Show' reads as if it had been taken down in shorthand from the lips of the veritable Polly, it is so life-like and interesting."

From the late Alexander Craig Gibson, Esq., F.S.A., with a presentation copy of his admirable work on *The Folk-Speech of Cumberland and some Districts adjacent*.—"With the Author's kind regards to Mrs. G. M. Tweddell, in whom he is gratified to have discovered a congenial taste."

6

From Mr. William Andrews, F.R.H.S., Author of *The History of the Dunmore Flitch*, &c.—" I am very much pleased with Mrs. Tweddell's volume, and so are all those who have seen it. Though I like all the pieces, the poem on ' T' Awd Cleveland Customs ' delights me most."

From Mr. F. K. Robinson, Author of *A Glossary of Yorkshire Words and Phrases, collected in Whitby and the Neighbourhood; Whitby: its Abbey, and the principal parts of the Neighbourhood,* &c.—" Florence Cleveland is very happy in her North Yorkshire productions. She has both an eye and an ear for its picturesque and expressive Dialect."

From Louis H. Phillips, Esq., Barrister-at-Law.—" I have to thank you very much for Mrs. Tweddell's most interesting book, which I have just finished reading. It is really a refreshing and agreeable contribution to the local literature of the day; and you may take my compliment (such as it is worth) as the more sincere in that I am no admirer of *local*, by which I mean *dialect*, verses or sketches as a rule I admit their *value* in their place, for special and antiquarian purposes; but, as Johnson said about wines, ' they are not for me.' If the book had not been your wife's, probably I should not have looked at it. As it is, I own myself rewarded."

From Mrs. Macquoid, Authoress of *Forgotten by the World, Hester Kirton, By the Sea, Doris Barugh,* &c.—" Please thank Mrs. Tweddell for the pleasure her verses have given us. Some of them are very pretty."

The above are selected from scores of others, from all classes of persons. The following London and provincial publications have also commended the work, viz.—The Archæologist, the Barnsley Chronicle, the Barnsley Times, the Bradford Chronicle, the Chelsea Times, the City Press, the Criterion, the Derbyshire Courier, the Durham Advertiser, the Durham Chronicle, the Eastern Morning News, the Freemason, the Gisbrough Exchange, the Harrogate Gazette, the Hull News, the Hull Packet, Iron, the Knaresbro' Times, the Leamington Courier, the Leeds Mercury, Lloyd's Weekly London Newspaper, the Masonic Magazine, the Middlesbrough Exchange, the Middlesbrough News, the Middlesbrough and Stockton Gazette, the Middlesbrough Temperance Visitor, the Newcastle Daily Chronicle, the Northern Echo, the Otley News, the Pictorial World, the Sheffield Times and Iris, the South Durham Herald, the Sunderland Times, the Tadcaster Post, the Waikouaiti and Shag Valley Herald (Hawksbury, Province of Otago, New Zealand), the Wakefield Free Press, the Westminster Chronicle, the Wetherby News, the Whitby Gazette, the Whitby Times, the York Hera'd, the Yorkshire Gazette, the Yorkshire Post, and others.

Reduced from 1s. 6d. to 1s., or post free to any part of Great Britain or Ireland on receipt of fourteen penny postage stamps,

With a Map of the District on both sides of Tees Bay, the second edition, revised by the Author, of

THE VISITOR'S HANDBOOK TO REDCAR

COATHAM, AND SALTBURN-BY-THE-SEA,

With Historical and Descriptive Accounts of Places of Interest in the Neighbourhood suitable for Rambles.

By GEORGE MARKHAM TWEDDELL.

"I have received so much pleasure from its perusal and guidance through the Saltburn locality, that I consider it cheap at even double its price."—John Reed Appleton, Esq., F.S.A.

"This little book, which has reached its second edition, will find a welcome place in the knapsack of every traveller visiting the delightful retreats upon which it dilates. It is full of interesting and valuable information, historical and descriptive, which is given in the familiar and easy style so desirable and proper in productions of this nature. The author has availed himself largely of authorities bearing upon the subjects before him, but his quotations are well chosen for their direct applicability, and are connected in a happy and judicious manner. The poetical illustrations, drawn from some of our best poets, tend to diversify the character of the work, and, being everywhere exceedingly appropriate, they are by no means the least interesting features in this useful and entertaining little handbook, which may be safely recommended to the notice of all who take an interest in the charming locality of which it treats."—Middlesbro' News.

"Visitors to Redcar wish to know something about the antecedents of the place, and Mr. Tweddell has thrown many pleasing and antiquarian researches together to make a useful book for their information. The adjacent villages and things of note are treated of, and the attention of visitors called to many interesting places and objects which are noted in the neighbourhood. Mr. Tweddell has done the public service in printing a second edition of his interesting little work, which will not fail to please and be useful to all who read it."—Stockton Herald.

"The writer of this little volume has for many years been well known as the author of several works of considerable literary merit, amongst which that of 'Shakspere, his Times and Contemporaries,' is undoubtedly his best, and occupies no mean rank in the voluminous literature relating to the 'myriad-minded bard of Avon.' The reputation Mr. Tweddell has earned for himself by the work just mentioned is fully sustained in the present publication. Being a native of a locality adjoining that which he describes, and possessing an immense fund of local, antiquarian, topographical, and historical information, combined with mental gifts of a very high order, he was well qualified for the task he undertook in the production of a handbook to Redcar and its vicinity. The work shows evidences of a very entensive research for facts relating to the places he describes, which he has used in a most judicious manner. His descriptions are full and accurate, and a vein of genuine humour runs through the work, relieving it of that dull and tedious air which is so characteristic of works of this class. In short, it does much credit to the taste, industry, and ability of its author. Every visitor to Redcar or the neighbourhood should provide himself with this handbook, and thus secure one of the best of guides and companions for his rambles."—Stockton Gazette and Middlesbrough Times.

8

Milton Keynes UK
Ingram Content Group UK Ltd.
UKHW022029151223
434483UK00005B/175